Paperie

SIMON &
SCHUSTER
EDITIONS

Paperie

THE ART OF WRITING AND
WRAPPING WITH PAPER

Kate's Paperie with Bo Niles

Photography by Evan Sklar
Design by Eric Baker Design Associates

OTHER BOOKS BY BO NILES

TIMELESS DESIGN
WHITE BY DESIGN
LIVING WITH LACE
A WINDOW ON PROVENCE
THE NEW YORK BOOK OF TEA
HOMEPLAN
PLANNING THE PERFECT KITCHEN
MAKE YOURSELF AT HOME

SIMON & SCHUSTER EDITIONS
ROCKEFELLER CENTER
1230 AVENUE OF THE AMERICAS
NEW YORK, NEW YORK 10020

DESIGN BY TIKA BUCHANAN,
ERIC BAKER DESIGN ASSOCIATES

PROJECT MANAGED FOR KATE'S PAPERIE
BY NANCY FREMONT

MANUFACTURED IN CHINA

10 9 8 7 6 5 4 3 2 1

LIBRARY OF CONGRESS
CATALOGING-IN-PUBLICATION DATA
NILES, BO
    PAPERIE : THE ART OF WRITING
    AND WRAPPING WITH PAPER / KATE'S PAPERIE
    WITH BO NILES ; PHOTOGRAPHY BY EVAN SKLAR
        P. CM.
    INCLUDES INDEX.
    1. PAPER WORK. 2. PAPERMAKING.
    3. STATIONERY.
    I. KATE'S PAPERIE. II. TITLE
    TT870.N55 1999
    745.54—DC21
    98-33664 CIP
ISBN 0-684-84423-0

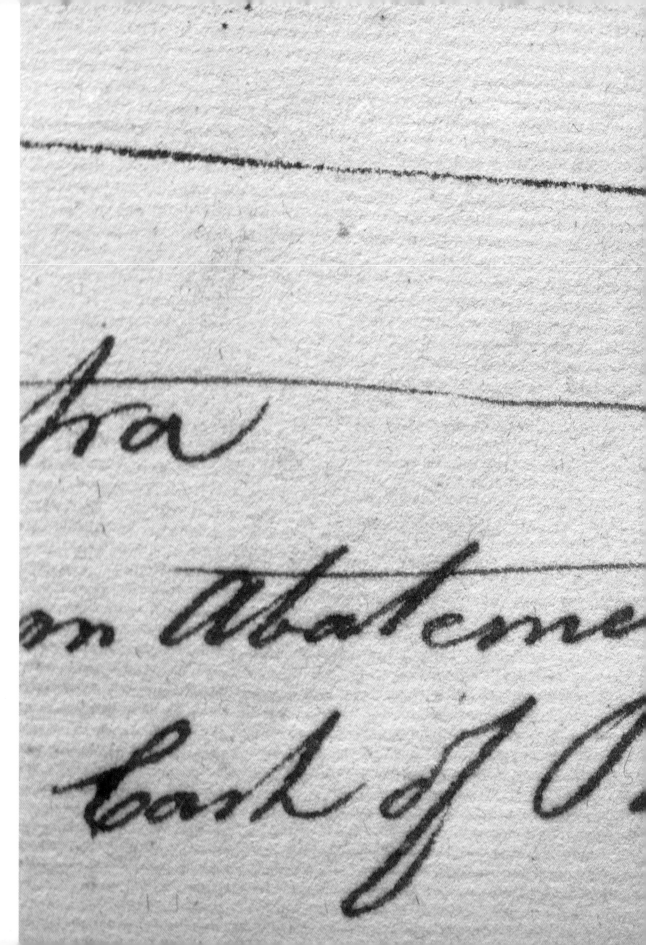

on Paper

Revere Esq

ACKNOWLEDGMENTS... WHEN WE FIRST IMAGINED A KATE'S PAPERIE BOOK, we had no idea of the circuitous journey we would soon be taking. We had a vision and a passion we wanted to share, but we never dreamed defining that passion would lead us to a new level of personal insight and a better understanding of our mission as a business.

We have so many to thank for their support and contributions. The realization of this book must be credited first and foremost to the staff and management of Kate's Paperie. The same energy and spirit that is responsible for our phenomenal growth was directed toward our book project from start to finish.

Our gratitude to Martha Kaplan for believing in us from the very beginning and guiding us through the complex world of publishing every step of the way. Martha led us to Janice Easton at Simon & Schuster. Janice deserves a tremendous amount of credit for her patience and foresight. She worked with us continually to find solutions without compromising our views.

Thank you to Bo Niles for her extensive research and constant endeavor to understand our vision. She was able to take all our disjointed thoughts, facts, and opinions and masterfully weave them into a fabric that has become this book. Kudos to Eric Baker and Tika Buchanan of Eric Baker Design Associates for doing a terrific job while suffering through our education in book design. The end result is beautiful. Thank you to Evan Sklar for his marvelous photographs.

We are grateful to Nancy Fremont for directing this project from the start. She was the glue that held the book together. She contributed content, style, wisdom, and compassion. She dealt with various temperaments of authors, designers, publishers, contributing artists, and papermakers to produce a wonderful book.

Finally, my most heartfelt thanks to the people in my life who gave me their love and made so many personal sacrifices on my behalf throughout the entire process. Thank you to my wife, Diana, for giving up my companionship for weeks on end and never complaining. Her love and support are my energy. Thank you to my sons, Eric and Tony, for believing in me. They helped me look beyond myself and share with others. A special thank you to Leonard Flax, who taught me true friendship and business partnership can truly coexist.

contents

2700 B.C. Invention of Chinese characters 2200 Oldest extant manuscript on papyrus 1035 Earliest mention of packaging, for food wrappers in Egypt 200 Introduction of parchment A.D.105 Invention of paper 400 Invention of true ink, from lampblack 400 Paper used "universally" in China 610 Paper introduced into Japan from China 700 Introduction of sizing on paper 751 Paper made in Samarkind 770 Earliest printed papers, the Million Dharani Prayers commissioned by Empress Shotoku 868 Earliest printed book, **The Diamond Sutra** 1041 Invention of moveable type, in China 1109 Earliest existing European manuscript on paper, a deed written in Arabic and Greek, from Sicily 1116 Earliest stitched books, from China 1151 Stamping mill founded in Spain 1154 First mention of paper in Italy 1282 Introduction of watermarks in Italy 1403 Invention of metal moveable type, in Korea; six years later, first book printed with moveable type in America 1423 Origins of block printing in Europe 1450 Gutenberg produces his Forty-Two-Line Bible 1470 Earliest printed poster, a bookseller's advertisement is produced 1501 Invention of roman-style type 1550 Wallpaper introduced into Europe from China, by Dutch and Spanish traders 1590 Introduction of marbled papers into Europe from Persia 1609 Earliest newspaper with regular publication dates, in German 1638 First printing press set up in America, in Cambridge, Mass. 1680 Invention of the Hollander Beater, in The Netherlands 1690 First paper money issued in the American colonies 1690 First paper mill established in America, near Philadelphia 1704 Earliest permanent newspaper in America, produced in Boston 1714 Invention and patent of the typewriter, in England 1719 French scientist Reamur suggests wood as a papermaking fiber, after studying wasps' nests 1720 Invention of glazing rolls for finishing paper 1764 Invention of coating paper, in England 1775 First true American banknote, designed and engraved by Paul Revere 1780 Earliest use of steel-nib pens for writing, superseding quill pens 1790 Invention of hydraulic press, in England 1798 Invention of lithography, in Germany 1798 Invention of paper machine, in France; earliest patented paper machine appeared three years later, in England 1806 Patent taken out by Fourdriner for his paper machine; improved version of machine operates commercially in 1812, in England 1810 First steam-powered press, in England 1832 First patent for a "self-filling" pen 1847 First postage stamps used in America 1850 Introduction of the paper bag 1856 Discovery of aniline dyes 1868 Typewriter is patented 1880 Invention of linotype and monotype 1885 Invention of the practical fountain pen 1894 Automation of machines to make paper boxes launches "packaging era" 1907 Introduction of kraft paper, in Canada 1921 Invention of teleprinter 1934 Largest sheet of handmade paper ever formed, measuring 200-inch square, in Japan 1938 Invention of the ball-point pen 1944 Automatic sequence controlled calculator, or Marc 1 Computer, designed by Howard Aiken 1954 Fortran, first computer programming language developed 1965 Computer typesetting introduced, in Germany 1971 Bell Lab's Dennis Ritchie produces most widely used general-purpose language for programmers 1973 Teletext pioneered, in Britain 1976 First Apple computer introduced 1976 Fax machine comes into widespread use 1983 Introduction of cell phones 1984 First Macintosh computer introduced 1984 Pulp spraying becomes popular for forming large sheets of paper without the need for enormous vats 1985 Rising popularity of, and demand for, handmade papers 1990 Introduction of the first 100 percent cotton recycled paper, Crane's Crest R 1995 U.S. currency redesigned with watermarked paper 1998 Crane introduces Continuum, a line of tree-free papers made with industrial hemp.

A BRIEF HISTORY

introduction

"ONLY A SCRAP OF PAPER!
A SOMETHING MADE FROM
RAGS AND REFUSE—
AND YET HOW MUCH IT SIGNIFIES.
HAS ANYONE REFLECTED
WHAT THE WORLD
WOULD BE
WITHOUT PAPER"

THE BERLIN AND JONES ENVELOPE CO.

Paper impacts virtually every facet of our lives.

Everywhere we look we are surrounded by things that are made from or printed on paper. At home there is the grocery list, the television schedule, the message pad next to the telephone, framed photos of loved ones, facial tissue, lamp shades, a stick'em note on the refrigerator, bank checks, a bookmark—to name just a few. Paper products fill an entire aisle in the supermarket, and myriad shops, not just Kate's Paperie, are dedicated to paper in various forms, from stationery to works of art. The list of paper goods we use daily could fill—yes—the pages of a book.

Paper dominates our daily routine. Most of us awaken to a cup of coffee and a newspaper. Office work involves dozens of communications on paper: letters, memos, lists, schedules. Some of these may be transmitted electronically, but most are still typed on paper, even if they end up being faxed rather than stamped and mailed, and many also are photocopied on paper for files or internal FYIs. For those who lunch at their desks, a sandwich from the deli is wrapped in paper "to go," with a side order of soup or coffee poured into a paper cup—or is "brownbagged" from home in just that, a kraft-paper bag.

Besides the stack of mail that piles up at the office, there is another that fills the mailbox at home. Daily, we sift through flyers, brochures, cards and letters, bills, and solicitations from charitable organizations. A mail-order package may await, with a special something wrapped in tissue within its cardboard box or padded mailing bag. From minute to minute, paper attracts or requires our attention.

Over twenty-five years ago, International Paper tagged its Strathmore art paper with the slogan: "Paper is part of the picture." It is. Paper is also part of history, and of education and learning, and of society. Paper is part of life. Paper documents our past and transmits our forecasts for the future. It says something about who and what we are. Where would the ideas of men and women be without paper? Their ideals? Their hopes? Their dreams? We are the measure of our words, and for the most part, words on paper.

Although pundits predict a paperless society and electronic devices appear to be taking over our lives, paper remains by far the most pervasive and expressive medium for communication. Indeed, the computer is rapidly making printers of all of us. Desktop publishing has opened up the field for self-taught printers who are creating their own stationery, their own party invitations, their own business cards. So, even as we become more attracted by the revolution in electronics, we increasingly rely on paper. No matter what we read off the screen, we seem to need that sensuous, tactile involvement with what we read and write.

When you lift a book such as this one, open it, flip through its pages, and perhaps even sniff it, you are experiencing paper in one of its most pleasurable forms. Run your fingers across the cover and its flyleaf, then caress the endpapers and pages; listen to the pages as you riffle them through your fingers. Paper is sensuous. Paper is something to revel in.

What we have learned over years in the business of purveying paper is that people are coming to appreciate paper more and more. Even if they seem to see more what is *on* the paper than what is *in* it, they are excited by paper and want to know more *about* it.

When you come into Kate's Paperie, you are surrounded by paper. We believe that one way to enhance one's enthusiasm for life is with paper. Paper can be, and often is, a statement of your personality and taste. The paper you choose to write on, wrap a gift in, or decorate your home with, says as much about you as the clothing you wear or the food you eat. Paper can be, and often is, a statement of your personality and taste.

Paper is a gracious and hospitable medium. It asks nothing of us but accedes to our wishes and desires. It allows itself to be folded, wadded, shaped, cut, shredded, torn. It receives inks, paint, pencil, charcoal, X-Acto blades, and scissors with equal equanimity. Paper brings out the best in us.

Paper has personality. Specific characteristics differentiate one paper from another. Paper has to be touched and held to be appreciated. You cannot know what paper to buy unless you feel its heft, test its weight, check its pliability, look up at it or through it to the light.

This book, in essence, is like Kate's Paperie—a microcosm of the world of paper. Our shop displays over forty thousand papers, many of them handmade, from over forty countries around the world. When a customer enters our shop, we are there to counsel and assist in the selection of paper: What kind of paper will work best for an invitation to a special occasion, such as a wedding or bar/bat mitzvah? What kind of paper should I choose to wrap a gift? Is one paper more suitable than another for making a lamp shade or covering a box—or even for making a box from scratch?

We answer hundreds of questions like these every day, about paper itself and also about all the wonderful things that enhance paper or that paper enhances—rubber stamps and sealing waxes, fountain pens and inks, writers' journals, artists' supplies, and ribbons and ties.

This book serves as a guide in much the same way. When you open this book and read on, it is as if you opened the door into Kate's Paperie. Within these pages we aim to demystify the more arcane aspects of construction, weight, and other properties of paper, and share with you what we know so that you can make informed and confident choices for any project you might dream of. We want you to love paper as much as we do.

Leonard Flax and Joe Barreiro

KATE'S PAPERIE

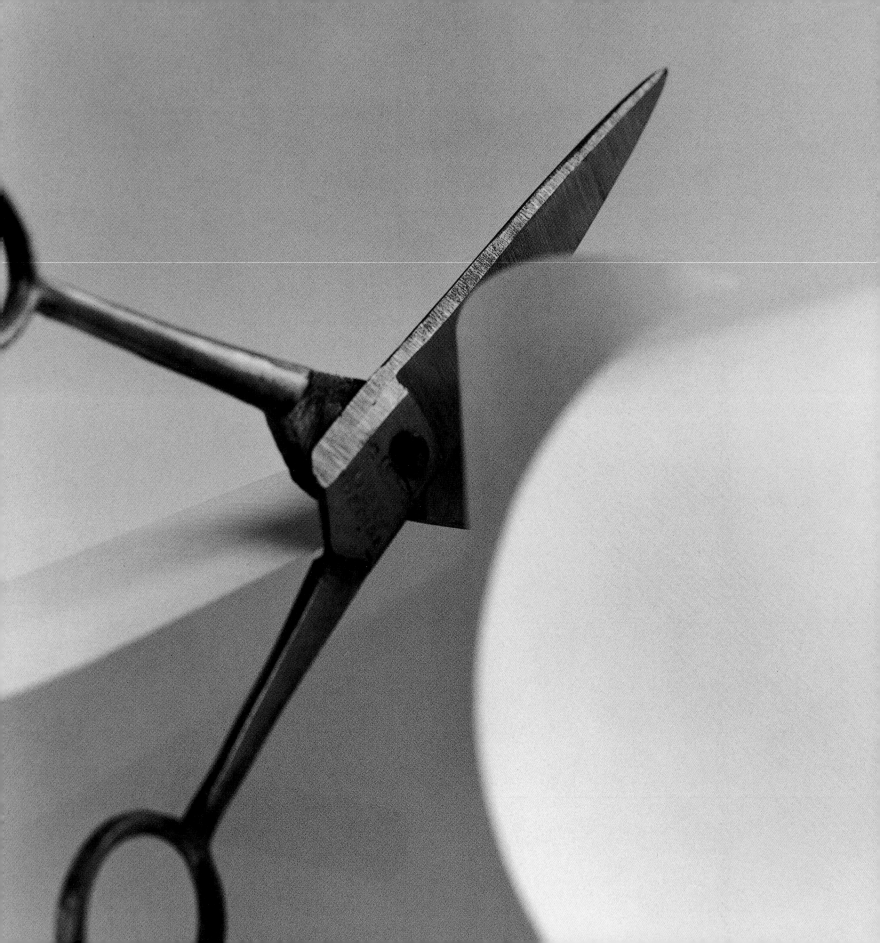

PAPER RECEIVES OUR THOUGHTS AND FEELINGS
WITH THE UTMOST EQUANIMITY AND CALM

transforming paper

PAPER TRANSMITS OUR IDEAS,
COLLECTS OUR SECRETS
PAPER ACCEPTS US FOR WHAT WE ARE
AND EXPRESSES
WHAT WE HOPE
TO BE

Once paper was mass produced and could be afforded by anyone and everyone who wanted to write something down, it obviously became less valuable as a medium for expression—unless posterity dictated otherwise. As these doodles reveal, people now felt they could risk setting whatever they were thinking about down on paper.

Writing transforms paper from a *tabula rasa* into a vital form of communication. We speak in words. We think in words. What we think, say, and feel cannot be preserved indefinitely without being recorded in some manner. Writing was invented to state facts and perpetuated to relay information and ideas. Because early peoples were profoundly religious,

From Japan, the craft of papermaking traveled westward across the Gobi Desert to Central Asia via the Silk Route that would eventually be mapped out by Marco Polo. By A.D. 751, paper was being made in Samarkand from the flax and hemp that grew in abundance along its irrigation canals; within forty years paper reached Baghdad. Paper finally found its way across the Mediterranean Sea into southern Spain with that country's conquest by the Moors in the eleventh century. One hundred years later, the Crusaders carried paper into Sicily and Italy, from whence it spread northward into the rest of Europe. At this point, over a thousand years had passed since its invention.

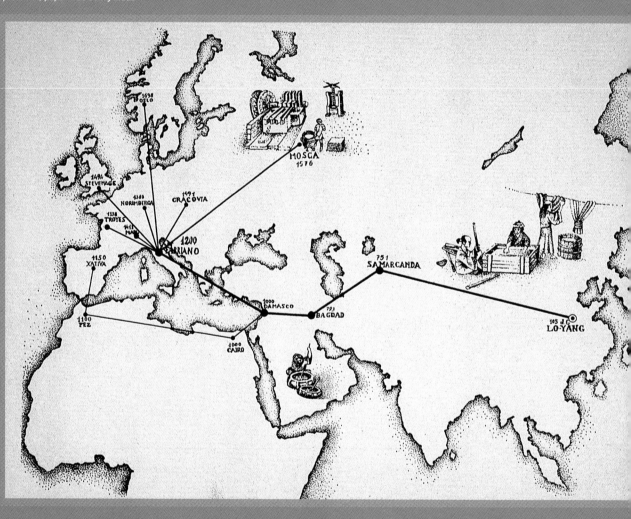

if not superstitious, writing was also relied on to disseminate sacred edicts and creeds. Writing is vital as a form of communication, and vital as a repository of the details of our lives as human beings upon this earth. It is also a medium for expressing our heart's desires. We are what we write.

The history of writing preceded that of paper by many centuries. Although scholars believe writing was innovated around 6000 B.C., no records exist of man's earliest efforts. Writing developed independently in different areas of the world. Sumerians wrote in cuneiform, a system of slashlike lines that evolved from pictograms, or simplified drawings, that represented ideas and objects in syllable form. Aztecs also used pictograms. Mayans as well as Egyptians communicated through hieroglyphs, a more sophisticated form of picture writing. Once signs and symbols began to be abstracted to represent the phonetics of the spoken language rather than the way of how objects looked, it was only a matter of time before such signs were formalized into an alphabet. Alphabets radically reduced the number of signs necessary to transmit ideas. It was the Phoenicians who developed the first recognizable alphabet, which contained only consonants. The Greeks added vowels. (By contrast, the Chinese never developed a written language based on phonetics; the signs and symbols that make up the Chinese characters known today number in the thousands.)

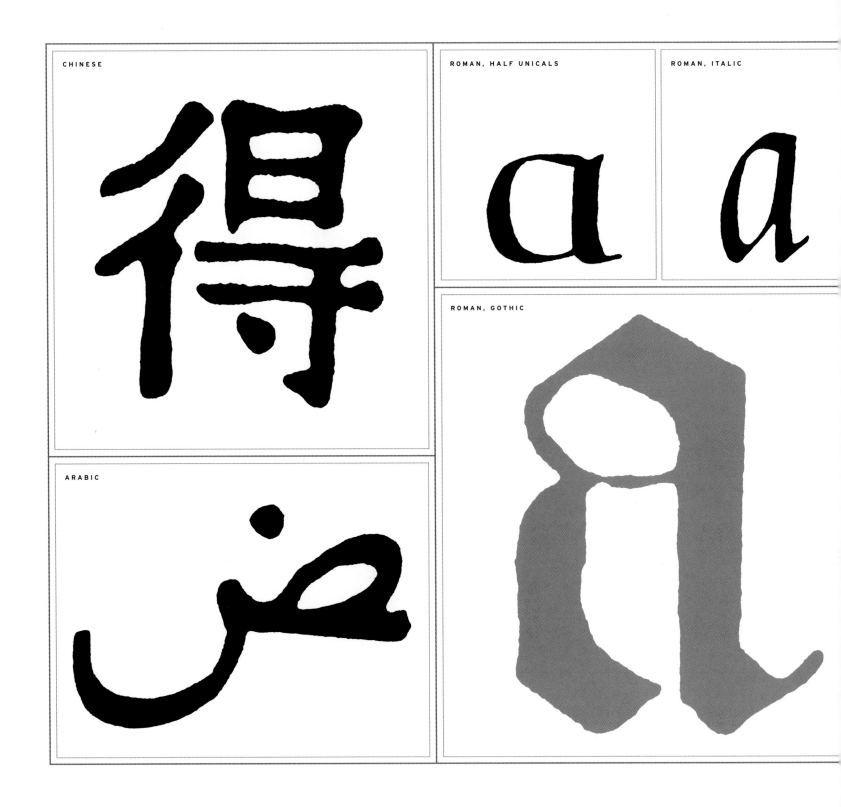

CHINESE

ROMAN, HALF UNICALS

ROMAN, ITALIC

ROMAN, GOTHIC

ARABIC

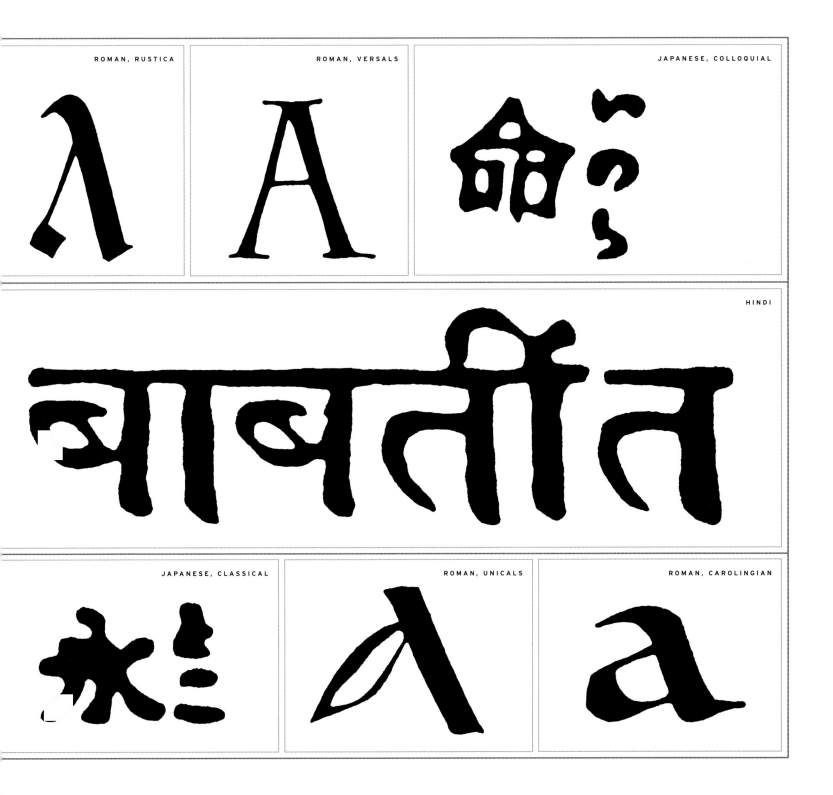

Prior to paper—and its precursors papyrus and parchment—there were several media for communication. Clay tablets could be incised or stamped and passed from hand to hand. Stone was chiseled; metal, scratched. Cloth and the bark and leaves of various plants and shrubs were also used. Depending upon the medium, writing was articulated with sharp pieces of wood, bone, or reed (called styluses) or marked by sharpened reeds dipped into an inklike substance made from soot, resin, and water.

Many things that influence our lives originated in China. Paper is but one of these. The earliest acount of a paper-like substance, from around 200 B.C., describes a scrap of cob-webby tangled silk; a dictionary of Chinese characters dating from A.D. 69 defines inscribed strips of bamboo (and sometimes silk) by the character *chih*. *Chih*, however, was not true paper. The invention of the material we might recognize as a true paper is credited to Ts'ai Lun, a eunuch in the court of Emperor Ho Ti, in A.D. 105. Given the task of reorganizing the imperial library, Ts'ai Lun conceived of a flat, lightweight, compact replacement for the wooden tablets and chih documents stacked throughout the space: a thin sheet of matted fiber made from a beaten mixture of hemp, rags, fishnet, and bark and composed upon a mold. Awarded the patents on his invention, Ts'ai Lun initiated the production of paper for the written records that were required by the bureaucracy. For hundreds of years the knowledge of paper remained within Chinese borders. With their invention of brushes and ink, and using the characters they already knew, the Chinese started writing on paper. The finest examples of the calligraphy they developed record the sayings of Confucius and other religious writings.

It is said that the written language was imported into Japan by Atogi, a son of the king of Korea, in the third century A.D. By the seventh century, China was actively engaged in an educational

HEBREW NAMES	EARLIEST SIGNS	SEMITIC				GREEK					ETRUS		LATIN	
		EARLY PHOEN 1200 B.C.	EARLY HEBREW 857 B.C.	MOAB 842 B.C.	PHOEN 8TH CENT B.C.	EARLY 9TH-7TH CENT B.C.	EAST 6TH CENT B.C.	WEST 6TH CENT B.C.	CLASSIC 403 B.C.	MODERN GREEK LETTERS	MARSILIANA 6 CENT B.C.	CLASSIC 400 B.C.	EARLY 4TH CENT B.C.	CLASSIC A.D. 100
ALEPH (oxhead)										alpha				
BETH (house)										beta				
GIMEL (throwing stick)										gamma				
DALETH (door)										delta				
HE (man)										epsilon				
WAW (nail or peg)														
													CG	G
ZAYIN										ʒeta				
HETH (twisted string)										eta				
TETH (geometric sign)										theta				
YOD (hand)										iota				
												introduced later		
KAPH (branch)										kappa				
LAMED (oxgoad)										lambda				
MEM (water)										mu				
NUN (snake)										nu				
SAMEKH (fish)										xi				
AYIN (eye)										omnicron				
PE (mouth)										pi				
SADHE (snare?)														
Q'OPH (monkey)														
RESH (human head)										rho				
SHIN (mountain peak)										sigma				
TAW (mark or brand)										tau				
										upsilon				
												introduced later		
										chi				
						phi	psi	omega	digamma					
												introduced later		

The basic methodology for making paper by hand has changed hardly at all in the two thousand years, since paper was invented in China. When you stop and think about it, this comes as no surprise, for both the ingredients and the recipe are simple in the extreme. The evolution of written language and alphabets, by contrast, is quite complex and shows marked differences in different parts of the world. Western alphabets can be traced to signs and symbols that were abstracted by the Phoenicians from primitive pictograms. As these alphabets evolved, they assimilated idiosyncrasies specific to their particular culture. Our letters take their cue from the classic, chiseled Roman alphabet.

exchange with Japan. Japanese scholars traveled through the Korean peninsula to the mainland to study a wide range of disciplines spanning the arts and sciences, agriculture, philosophy, and medicine. Taking the reverse route, a number of Chinese missionaries transported written pages into Korea, and thence into Japan. It was a Korean Buddhist

monk, Doncho, who, as chief physician and adviser to the empress of Japan, introduced the compatible skills of ink making and papermaking to that country; both quickly secured a foothold in Japanese culture. Doncho's influence over the empress was enormous, culminating in a vast commission—the printing of over 1 million Buddhist prayer charms, called *dharani*. The undertaking took over six years to complete, using many tiny woodblocks, and marked, in 770, the first instance in the world of printing on paper. This is also the first example of mass production of any product anywhere.

The term "paper" derives from the Greek and Latin words for papyrus, a reed with a tassel-like head that once grew profusely along the Nile Delta. In its heyday around 2000 B.C., Egyptian papyrus was used for virtually everything, from lightweight skiffs to shrouds for the mummified dead; parts of the plant were even eaten. In fact, papyrus was so ubiquitous and so indispensable to the rituals and routines of Egyptian life—and death—that the hieroglyph depicting papyrus was also the symbol for Lower Egypt.

Papyrus grew tall, to between thirteen and eighteen feet, but usually only the bottommost two feet of the cane, or stem, were reserved for papermaking. The rind was cut off and the pith inside sliced into strips, which were rolled and soaked until softened. The strips were then unrolled and laminated—side by side for the lower layer, perpendicularly for the top layer—to form a sheet (the Romans, who imported papyrus, called this a *plagula*). This sheet was soaked again, possibly bound with a wheat paste, then hammered flat and

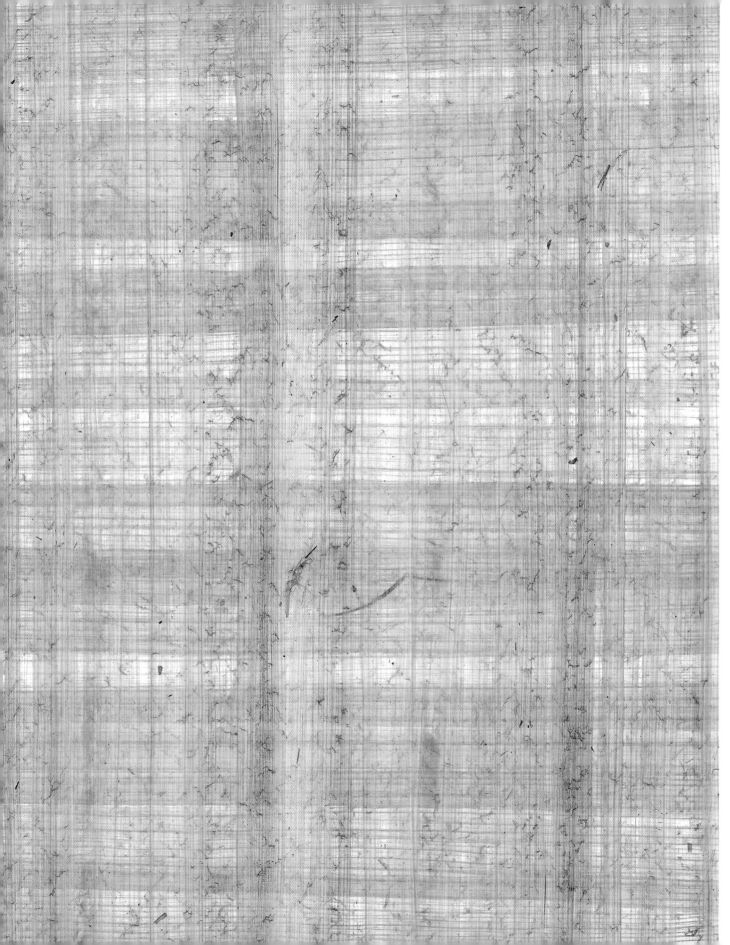

At the Tashilungpo Monastery at Xigatse, high in the Himalayan mountains of Tibet, half a dozen Buddhist monks work together to print Buddhist scriptures for prayer books to be used in their monastery. The monks print these scriptures by placing sheets of paper over inked woodblocks that they rub with rollers. A cord or metal spike keeps the many leaves of a book in their correct order.

left to dry in the sun. To smooth its surface, it was scoured and burnished with a shell. When a document required more space than a single sheet could accommodate, several sheets would be pasted together end-to-end to form a scroll, which could then be rolled up and carried on a wooden rod. A typical scroll measured twenty sheets in length. The finest, smoothest sheet was reserved for the top, or outside, of the scroll; sheets of lesser grades were rolled inside, to protect them from damage. Because of its portability, the papyrus scroll was adopted as a medium for communication in lands with which Egypt traded, including Assyria, Greece, and the Roman Empire.

Papyrus-based documents and texts on scrolls were disseminated throughout the ancient Mediterranean until the fourth century A.D., when papyrus was superseded by parchment. A number of disadvantages marked the scroll format: it was difficult to find one's place in the text; papyrus could be written on one side only; and lengthy texts were cumbersome to carry.

Parchment, which originated in Pergamum, the city for which it is named, is made from stretched, untanned animal skin, which is far more durable than fragile papyrus. Although a number of different animals could provide the hides for parchment, most hides were secured from sheep and goats. The thinnest, whitest, and most prized specimen was pearlskin, which was stretched from the uterine wall of a stillborn or newborn female kid. The skin for all parchment underwent a number of steps to render it smooth enough to write on. An initial soaking with lime for up to two weeks loosened the animal hair so that it could be scraped off. A second washing softened the skin until it was pliable enough to stretch over a frame, where it dried until taut. After a second scraping, the skin was dusted with chalk and/or rubbed with pumice stone to prepare the surface for writing.

Because the flesh side is whiter and less coarse than the hair side of a skin, earliest efforts focused on preparing only the flesh side for writing. With the invention of the multiple paged *codex*, the forerunner to the book, parchment began to be written on both sides. When pages were folded, flesh side was matched with flesh side and hair side with hair side to achieve optical harmony.

Because parchment is as smooth and long-lasting as the goat or lambskin from which it is made, it has never disappeared as a medium for preserving an important piece of text. Parchment—or finer, paler vellum—is used for diplomas and other documents that are expected to outlast one's lifetime. At Kate's Paperie, we stock parchments in a number of weights because we have found that people love to work with them when they want to create an individual artwork that might entail a thick, resilient alternative to paper. Parchment is also a wonderful medium for an invitation to a special event.

In our computer age, many people seem to write with greater comfort and alacrity on a keyboard, in front of a computer screen, than at a table with pen in hand. Even so, we at Kate's Paperie take heart in the fact there is a countertrend: more and more people seem to take pleasure and pride in how and what they write. Nothing is more charming than a handwritten note. Nothing gives greater pleasure than a letter penned by hand. Nothing is accorded more respect than a personal reminder affixed to a business card. Paper and pen still

hold their magic. We still entrust them with our dearest wishes and innermost thoughts and dreams. The art of writing will never disappear. It will never go out of style.

For centuries, the art of writing was, indeed, an art—and one that was considered sacrosanct. In post-Roman Europe, many believed the knowledge of letters and their graceful execution to be divinely ordained, because most writing (other than records of transactions) was executed by holy men/scribes whose main function was to transcribe, or copy, sacred texts. When Charlemagne, king of the Franks and emperor of the West, consolidated much of Christian Western Europe under his control at the end of the eighth century, he championed education and the development of calligraphic skills at the monasteries throughout his domain. (The term "calligraphy" combines the Greek words *kallos*, beauty, and *graphōes*, writing.) Although Charlemagne, like virtually everyone at the time, was illiterate (he simply added a cross to official documents signed by proxy), he mandated a uniform system of writing. He commissioned a team headed by one Alcuin of York to design an alphabetical script, which became known as the Carolingian hand.

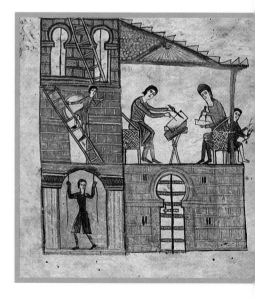

The room dedicated to the transcription of texts—the scriptorium—was set up near the monastery library. Here the monks sat in rows behind tilted desks, diligently working at their individual assignments. The monastery attempted to keep the scriptorium as warm as possible so that the writing would not be impeded. What with preparing the sheet of parchment (or vellum), trimming goose quills, constantly refilling quills with ink—and required breaks for prayers—a talented copyist could be expected to complete about three or four manuscript pages in a day.

Quill pens, cut and tapered from the outer feathers of geese, were used from the sixteenth century until the mid-nineteenth century. Goose quills retained an almost mystical aura; they were to be taken from the five best wing feathers shed during molting. Quills were first soaked to prepare them for cutting. The end of the quill was then sliced at an angle, and slit partway down its middle. Afterward, the nib was shaved, or beveled, to the shape needed to easily write a particular letterform, such as the Carolingian hand mentioned earlier or the Gothic script favored for many illuminated manuscripts.

The layout of the page was dictated by the size of the sheet of vellum and by the subject matter of the text. Devotional texts, such as Bibles and Psalters, ran a double column; classical texts (Greek and Roman works, such as natural histories) followed a single-block layout. Both formats were bordered by wide margins and highlighted by large initials, some of which were illuminated or illustrated with miniature paintings and gold leaf. Words penned in red ink served as cues to points in the text. The illuminated embellishments tended to be executed by laymen, and many a fine artist of the day practiced his hand at this refined form of painting.

Placing his parchment on a tilted, lecternlike desk, the scribe painstakingly set up his page layout with guidelines and indentations for any anticipated illuminated or red-penned initials. Once he had copied the prototype set before him, he indicated the initial for the illuminator by means of a tiny letter called a director. The creation of any ornament followed a step-by-step process: First, the design or motif was faintly sketched in with a stylus; then it was outlined in ink. Details were penned in, and the design was filled in with paint. Lastly, gold leaf might be applied.

With the invention of the printing press and the wider dissemination of books and of paper, more and more people became literate and felt they could communicate in their own hand, not through the services of a scribe. The role of the scribe faded into obscurity except for special assignments, such as the creation of a document. Instead, masters of the calligraphic arts were consulted for the development of typefaces, or fonts, for the nascent publishing industry; some of these masters taught penmanship, while others became engravers, printers, and, by default, publishers.

As teaching aids, manuals and copybooks began to be printed geared to those interested in learning fine penmanship. The first writing manual on record, *La Operina* (1524), was penned, then printed, by Ludovico degli Arrighi, a scribe in the papal chancery who set up his own press. A writing manual provided instruction, not only in the precise forming of letters but also in sitting at the desk, in cutting the quill, and in holding the pen. For those seeking personal instruction, a penman or writing master, with manual in hand, could be retained to guide the student through each pen stroke. Tracing letters directly

from the page became a common practice. Many a quill pen tore the page, or pages were removed altogether for practice sheets; for these reasons, few early writing manuals survive in good condition.

Modifications of the original chancery script, called *bastarda*, slowly evolved into a more fluid cursive script, and finally into a round hand that could be penned swiftly with few undue hesitations. John Ayres, active in England from 1680 until 1700, demonstrated a particularly fluent penmanship; by the eighteenth century his hand was the accepted norm throughout Europe.

Until writing manuals and instruction in penmanship became available in the United States, early Americans relied on itinerant penmen to transcribe their important deeds and documents. Once established, penmanship flourished as an accomplishment of which any educated person could be proud. But the flourishes and furbelows of even the most adroit hand slowed a writer down. Realizing this, a young businessman, Austin Norman Palmer, devised a system of handwriting that by 1900 had become the norm for all Americans. Combining instruction on correct posture and on holding the pen with exercises in which letters were traced and copied over and over on the page and blackboard, the Palmer method of penmanship was a required subject of study in every public school.

In China and Japan, calligraphy actively engages the mind, body, and spirit and (like yoga) is guided by rhythmic breathing. Throughout the breath, the calligrapher strives to achieve a balance of *sei* and *bi*—of accuracy and beauty. Since the eighth century, the Chinese have linked calligraphy intimately with poetry and painting, calling them the Three Perfections. In Japan, the items used to create calligraphy—brush, ink stick, inkstone, and paper—are known as the Four Treasures. Today as of old, handmade paper—and particularly a thick, creamy type called *hosho*—is the medium of choice for most Japanese calligraphers. *Hosho* responds ideally to india ink and allows the brush to move freely down the sheet. The Japanese speak of the brush in almost balletic terms, extolling its soaring leaps and the interludes when it is poised in stillness and silence. Calligraphy is both a form of exercise and a form of meditation.

The daughter of a master calligrapher and poet, Koho Yamamoto has practiced calligraphy from an early age. After studying with the late master of calligraphy Chiura Obata at the art school Obata ran at the Topaz Detention Center in Utah (where a number of West Coast Japanese were sequestered during World War II), she came to New York and established her reputation as a fine artist. In work-shops conducted in her studio in Soho, Koho Yamamoto, as **sensei**, or teacher, passes along the fine points of Notan—"the art of achieving dark and light tones on white Sumi-E paper with a single brush-stroke." Besides the calligraphic image demonstrated here, the single brushstroke method can be applied to paintings of bamboo, pine, plum blossoms, and land-scapes, among other subjects.

REPRESENTS THE BEGINNING OF A TRANSPORT OF ENERGY THAT WILL THE DEEPEST PART OF HIMSELF, HIS TRUE PATH....HIS WHOLE BODY MUST PARTICIPATE IN THE CALLIGRAPHIC PROCESS AND MUST FUNCTION IN HARMONY WITH HIS SPIRIT....HIS BODY WILL BECOME WEIGHTLESS, HIS HAND WILL GROW WINGS, WHILE HIS MODE OF EXPRESSION WILL BECOME MORE PROFOUND AND TRUER TO HIMSELF."

—HASSAN MASSOUDY, **ON ISLAMIC CALLIGRAPHY** (1986)

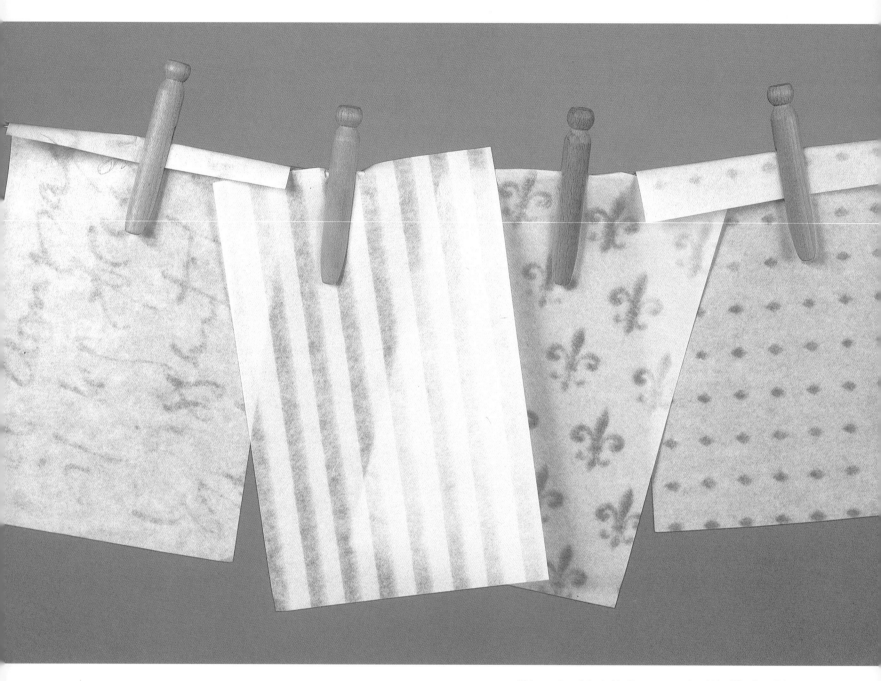

Watermarks originated in Europe as marks of identification. This clothespinned quartet of machine-made papers takes the concept further. Here, watermarking was utilized to create patterns in the papers that capitalize on the idea of juxtaposing areas of translucency and opacity. The effect is both delicious and visually arresting.

The craft of papermaking has changed hardly at all since paper was invented in A.D. 105. Anyone can make a sheet of paper. At Kate's Paperie, papermaking kits fly out of the store. The formula for any and every paper, be it a lovely, luxury handmade paper or a roll of newsprint manufactured by machine, is essentially the same: a slurry of fibrous material mixed with water and a bonding agent—and, perhaps, a sizing to seal the surface for printing or writing. Because paper can be made from many things—from cotton or linen rags, from wood or bark, even

During the Renaissance, paper began to be made and used in greater and greater quantities. One prolific correspondent was the artist Michelangelo Buonarroti; some of his letters, such as this one penned to "Nicholo," are preserved in the Laurentian Library in Florence, which he designed and which houses some of his most famous sculptures. As this letter illustrates, Michelangelo's mastery of penmanship was as accomplished as his skills as artist, sculptor, architect, and poet.

from cornstalks—you will have to consider a number of qualities, not just the way it looks, when you choose a paper for a particular purpose.

By the end of the Renaissance, printing presses and papermaking operations had been established in many cities throughout Europe. Paper was already being distinguished by function: high-quality white paper was reserved for documents and correspondence, and a lesser-grade white paper for books; brown paper, sold in bundles, was used for wrapping, and coarse, gray, unsized papers for blotting. No matter what the quality, though, all paper was made from rags.

Because beating the pulp to separate the fibers in the rags used for making paper is the most arduous task in the entire process, various methods were explored to speed up the procedure. At first, heavy axle-driven hammers stamped the pulp within a trough sluiced by fresh running water. Several sets of hammers were employed; some had spikes, which helped fray whole cloth. In the early eighteenth century, the hammers were replaced by a cylindrical beater fitted with blades, called a hollander. Invented by the Dutch, the hollander lacerated the rags as they passed over a stone or metal bedplate at the bottom of an oblong tub, significantly reducing beating time.

Unlike in Japan, where the best handmade papers were (and are) made with freezing water, in Europe the pulp-water mix, called stuff, was warmed. Once the pulp was macerated, it was kept afloat, by a mechanical agitator called a hog. The vat man formed a sheet of paper upon a mold with a removable sievelike frame called a deckle. (*Deckle* is a German term for "cover.") He shook the mold up and down and from side to side to distribute the fibers over the surface of the screen. The deckle was then passed to a coucher, who tipped the sheet over onto a pile of sheets, each separated by a piece of felt. After 144 sheets were counted out, the stack, called a post, was placed in a screw press; a thick board was set atop the stack, then the screw rotated with a lever to extract excess moisture. The lay man removed the sheets to another stack, minus the felt, where they were again submitted to pressure, gentler this time. He moved the sheets from press to press to achieve a smooth surface before the sheets were finally slung over ropes to dry. Dry sheets were dipped in a size with a gelatinous liquid made from animal bone and hoof, then dried again. Sizing ensured that the paper could be written on without the ink spreading or being absorbed into the paper. Burnishing was the final stage, to render as smooth a surface as possible.

The most significant advance in papermaking occurred early in the nineteenth century, with the invention of a machine that could produce a continuous web of paper, exclusive of hand labor. A pair of London stationers, Henry and Sealy Fourdrinier, working with a mechanic, Bryan Donkin, created a machine based on a French prototype; the descendants of their machine bear their name. (Later innovations included the heated drying cylinder and a cutting machine, both invented by Thomas Bonsor Crompton in 1820.) In a fourdrinier press, the web of paper passed over and under a series of cylinders, or rollers, which would form and flatten the paper as they extracted moisture from the resulting roll.

The oldest continuously operating paper mill in the world is located near the hill town of Gubbio, an hour or so north of Rome. Established in 1286, Fabriano has produced papers for many purposes, from papers for fine arts and printmaking to book stock to paper dedicated to photocopiers and scanners. Today, their operations, all located close to the original mill, include a press measuring over one hundred yards long that concentrates on commercial and high-technology paper orders, as well as small-run presses that produce 100 percent cotton-rag, mold-made, acid-free watercolor papers and stationery. They also continue to make handmade papers in the traditional manner. Of all their innovations, the watermark is the best known.

When you hold a sheet of paper to the light you will undoubtedly notice the translucent impression a watermark makes. The watermark identifies the maker of the paper and is considered a guarantee

Paper mills have always had to be located adjacent to copious supplies of running water. In a 1568 woodcut OPPOSITE by Jost Amman of Frankfurt of a vat man at work creating a sheet of paper, the water wheel is just barely visible through the open windows of the mill. As the vat man tends his mold, a young apprentice carries off a stack of damp sheets to a press, where they will be squeezed to rid them of as much moisture as possible before being hung up to dry.

of authenticity, craftsmanship, and quality. Also called by the French name *filigranes*, watermarks are thought to have initially been inspired by just that—water dripping from the papermaker's fingers onto the sheet of paper, which left rings on the surface that were visible when held up to the light. The earliest watermark on record, one of Fabriano's dating to the end of the thirteenth century, outlines a rough papal cross with circles at each of its four points and another in the center.

The earliest watermarks functioned like cue cards to help illiterate papermakers recognize their own molds. The mark was made by sewing a thin wire onto the mesh screen in the mold; when pressure was exerted, the wet pulp spread around the wire leaving a thinner layer of paper, and thus the translucent impression that was visible only when the sheet was held to the light. The wire was sewn in mirror image so that it would read correctly when the sheet was pulled off the mold. The papermaker originally centered the watermark on the sheet, but now it is often found near an edge, where it won't interfere with whatever might occur on the sheet.

Watermarks have long assumed a number of forms, from geometric shapes to numerals and names to botanical images. The images might be interpreted literally or symbolically. Some early symbolic watermarks were created to communicate unspoken concepts during periods of religious unrest. Over time, some watermarks proved to be unusually popular: by 1600, almost three hundred different versions of the crown and one thousand of the hand or glove and of the chalice were in use throughout Europe.

Some watermarks identified certain sizes and qualities of paper, such as foolscap—represented by a jester's hat with bells. A presumed source for the term "foolscap" is an Italian term, *foglia capa*, which loosely translates as best or top leaves—a supposed reference to the finest sheets of papyrus or parchment used in antiquity.

Once wire could be soldered, not simply sewn, onto the screen in the press, more complex watermarks could be devised. Dies were developed that created irregularities in the surface of the screen, allowing the paper to build up in certain areas to create watermarks that were as sophisticated as paintings, even if void of color.

For machine-made paper, the screen was wrapped around a cylinder called the dandy roll, which was invented at the London-based firm of T. J. Marshall in 1826. The name came, charmingly, from the comment made by one of the Marshall workers upon sighting the results of this invention: "Isn't that a dandy!" Watermarking occurs as the damp web of paper passes under the dandy roll.

Today, most paper we come in contact with every day is machine made. Over the years, all sorts of substitutes for cotton rags have been examined, including straw, cornstalks, and even the cloth recovered from swaddled mummies. Of all candidates, debarked wood proved most suited to the task. Earliest experiments in papermaking with wood pulp typically mixed it with familiar rag fiber. As mills became more sophisticated, much or all of the rag content was eliminated. Rag began to be conserved for fine papers, such as stationery. Today, the label "rag paper" or "100 percent cotton" will signify this finer-quality paper.

According to Crane & Co., papermakers based in Dalton, Massachusetts, three types of watermarks may be used today in the creation of a custom watermark design. The most traditional, a wire type, results in translucent marks like those shown on these pages. An image recessed into the dandy roll, on the other hand, creates a shaded mark. The third type combines both translucent and shaded elements. One of Fabriano's marks ABOVE depicts the twins Romulus and Remus with their adoptive wolf mother—a symbol of the city of Rome. Looked at closely, Fabriano's watermarked sheet also barely reveals the pale vertical lines, called chain lines, made when the screen in the mold presses against the paper.

Americans consume billions of tons of paper every year. To meet our seemingly insatiable demand for newsprint, stationery, wrapping paper, currency, and myriad other types of paper, including paper to feed the facsimile, the photocopy machine, and computer printers and scanners, the production of machine-made papers is booming. Because countless acres of trees and countless gallons of water are consumed in the manufacture of pulp paper, the demand for recycled paper is burgeoning, too, in an effort to save our natural resources. As a countertrend, the demand for luxury papers made by machine in the traditional manner from 100 percent cotton rags is also growing.

At Crane & Co., cotton-rag and raw-cotton products such as linters and clippings go into a pulper, which mixes them with recycled material called broke stock. The beater saturates the fibers until the cellulose content interlocks and coheres; the resulting pulp is fed onto a screen and thence to the dandy roll, which compacts the fibers and adds a watermark. Excess water extracted throughout the process is captured, cleaned, and returned to the Housatonic River, which runs alongside the mill.

The first paper mill in America was established in 1690 in Germantown, Pennsylvania, by William Rittenhouse, a German-born papermaker, and William Bradford, a printer. A paper "famine" occurred during the American Revolution, but, by war's end, eighty to ninety mills were meeting the new republic's increased demands for pamphlets, broadsides, newspaper, and "papers for correspondence." Within two decades that number had more than doubled, to two hundred mills.

In America, where trees loomed in seemingly endless supply, the first ground-wood pulp mill dedicated to commercial use was established in 1867. From that date forward, wood pulp revolutionized the paper industry, allowing for the manufacture of a wide range of paper products. Papermaking machinery extracts fibers from debarked wood by grinding it, usually in concert with chemicals that help hasten the maceration of the wood. The resulting pulp, or stuff, contains lignin, a substance that causes paper to yellow. Most of the paper made from wood pulp, such as newsprint, is not intended to last, so the fact that wood contains lignin or that the paper might deteriorate is not an issue. To counteract the effect of lignin on papers consumers might plan to file or save, manufacturers began to add bleaches to whiten the paper, as well as other chemicals to help postpone its degeneration. Today archival-quality pulp paper is designated as "acid free."

As pulp passes through the rollers of the papermaking machine—some of the largest of these measure over two football fields in length—the fibers align in the direction they travel, thereby creating a grain. One way to ascertain grain is to rip out a newspaper clipping: the paper will tear easily in one direction, that of the grain; it will be difficult to tear in the opposite direction, which is against the grain. (By contrast, a handmade paper is "rough-shake," which means the fibers are distributed randomly across the screen and therefore have no grain. If you want to tear a handmade paper, you have to fold it, and possibly score it if it is thick.)

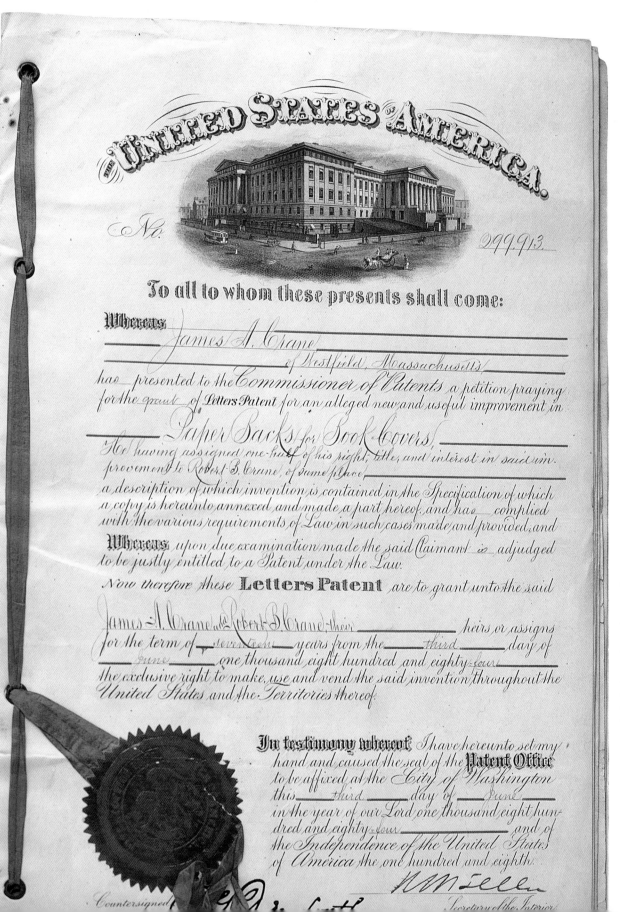

THE UNITED STATES OF AMERICA.

No. 299,913

To all to whom these presents shall come:

Whereas *James A. Crane* of *Westfield, Massachusetts,* has presented to the *Commissioner of Patents* a petition praying for the grant of *Letters Patent* for an alleged new and useful improvement in *Paper Backs for Book-Covers,* He having assigned one-half of his right, title, and interest in said improvement to *Robert B. Crane, of same place* a description of which invention is contained in the Specification of which a copy is hereunto annexed and made a part hereof, and has complied with the various requirements of Law in such cases made and provided, and

Whereas upon due examination made the said Claimant is adjudged to be justly entitled to a Patent under the Law.

Now therefore these **Letters Patent** are to grant unto the said *James A. Crane and Robert B. Crane their* heirs or assigns for the term of *seventeen* years from the *third* day of *June* one thousand eight hundred and eighty-four the exclusive right to make, use and vend the said invention throughout the United States and the Territories thereof.

In testimony whereof I have hereunto set my hand and caused the seal of the **Patent Office** to be affixed at the City of Washington this *third* day of *June* in the year of our Lord, one thousand eight hundred and eighty-four and of the Independence of the United States of America the one hundred and eighth.

Countersigned

Secretary of the Interior

In 1884, James Crane applied to the United States government patent office for a patent and permission "to make use and vend the said invention" for "an improvement in Paper Backs for Book Covers." Once the patent—no. 299913—was filled out, it was signed by the commissioner of patents and emblazoned with a wax seal to certify its authenticity.

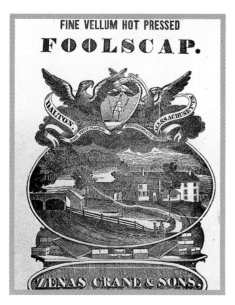

FINE VELLUM HOT PRESSED

FOOLSCAP.

ZENAS CRANE & SONS.

The manufacture of wood-pulp paper and the disposal of paper products after their use has long accounted for a huge proportion of the pollution in this country—from the wholesale cutting of trees to the chemical runoff issuing from mills into rivers and streams to the dumping of tons of paper in landfills. Environmental agencies and laws are attempting to redress the situation. Such agencies monitor and encourage companies to reduce pollution and waste—and recycling has become mandatory in many areas of the country.

Although pulp satisfies the need for mass-produced papers with a short lifespan, a taste for luxury papers, especially for social stationery, has never waned. At the same time, the demand for currency has always required a paper that would not deteriorate. Staking their reputation on both, Crane & Co., a family firm that operates four paper mills in northwestern Massachusetts, relies on cotton rags, not on tree pulp, as the base material for their papers.

Two hundred years ago, Zenas Crane set up the company's first, one-vat mill on the banks of the Housatonic River, across the state from his native Boston, in Dalton, Massachusetts. In doing so, he was following the lead of four generations of Cranes, who had been making paper since the early days of the Massachusetts Bay Colony. Zenas Crane's father had sold paper to engraver/silversmith Paul Revere in 1775 for the first true American banknotes to be issued in the colonies. This currency, a 36-shilling note depicting a patriot holding

Two wooden loft picks rest upon the screen of an antique paper mold. A loft pick was used to lift each damp custom-made sheet off the stack so that it could be positioned correctly on a rack in the drying loft. Once the sheet had dried, it was lifted off the rack, again with the loft pick, and placed atop the appropriate bundle of papers to prepare it for packing and shipping. (The wires in the screen can often be seen in thin, fine papers; the impressions they make are chain lines.) The Foolscap label is just one of the many Crane & Co. has employed over the years to identify its goods; the label depicts one of the early Crane mills. OVERLEAF Crane has made the paper for American banknotes for generations. Today, United States government regulations mandate that a dollar bill must be able to be folded and refolded nine thousand times before being removed from circulation.

a sword aloft, was designed and engraved by Revere. Crane & Co. continues to supply the paper for virtually all United States banknotes, as well as the currency paper for twenty-two other nations.

Banknotes are distinguished by a number of so-called enhancements unique to them, including the interweaving of subtle security threads, or filaments, among the paper fibers and/or the scattering of minute confettilike tissue disks, called planchettes, into the pulp. These precautions, along with watermarks, inhibit counterfeiting and forgeries. Because of these enhancements, as well as the continuous abuse to which a banknote is subjected as it is passed from hand to hand, banknotes have always been made of rag, not wood pulp. The formula for Crane's currency papers is a national secret.

Pulp made in the Crane mills is mixed from pure, 100 percent cotton waste recovered from ginning and textile manufacturing processes. The softest cottons received at the plant, reserved for Crane's social stationery, are the cuttings from T-shirts and BVDs. Softer still are the cotton linters recycled from the cottonseed industries; linters are the fuzz that remains stuck to the cottonseed after the boll is picked off. Cotton makes the best-quality paper for a number of reasons: it is naturally soft and bright and receives ink well; it is strong enough to withstand the most rigorous printing processes; it will endure for a long time; and, finally, recycled and recovered cotton is environmentally friendly because it is neither dumped nor wasted.

Today, Crane's stocks over a thousand varieties of 100 percent cotton writing papers and cards, including invitations and place cards hand bordered in silver or gold, business cards, résumé paper, letterhead, and social stationery, all of which may be custom engraved and watermarked.

At Crane's a number of different types of cards are still gilded by hand. The gilder bevels the edges and the curved corners of the stack of cards, making sure the angles of the beveled edges align precisely. The gilder then floats a whisper-thin sheet of gold leaf over the aligned edges of the cards and burnishes them, gently but firmly, so that the gold will adhere. Because it is valuable, excess gold (or silver or copper) is collected and recycled. A dandy roll OPPOSITE exhibits the watermark for one of the company's papers, called Crane's Crest.

"RAGS MAKE PAPER, PAPER MAKES MONEY,
MONEY MAKES BANKS, BANKS MAKE LOANS,
LOANS MAKE BEGGARS, BEGGARS MAKE RAGS."

ANONYMOUS (EIGHTEENTH CENTURY)

Today, a decent education guarantees that a student will read and write. Scanning the row upon row of volumes displayed in our nation's bookstores, it seems unbelievable that the desire to read is a fairly recent phenomenon. For centuries people counted on storytellers to perpetuate their myths. Customs and issues of behavior, too, tended to be passed along from one generation to the next by word of mouth. The advent

non fuisse ausum affirmare se raptū
in corpore sed dixisse. siue in corpore siue extra corp9 nescio deus scit. Hijs et
talibz argumentis apocriphas in libro ecclesie fabulas arguebat. Super
qua re lectoris arbitrio iudiciū derelin-
quens illud amoneo non haberi danielem apud hebreos inter prophetas.
sed inter eos qui agyographa conscri-
pserūt. In tres siquidē partes omnis
ab eis scriptura diuiditur: in legē in
prophetas et in agyographa id est
in quīqz et octo et undecim libros: de
quo nō est hui9 tēporis disserere. Que
aūt ex hoc prophetā. ymmo contra hūc
librū porphirius obiciat testes sunt
methodi9 eusebius apollinaris: qui
multis versuū milibz eius vesanie re-
spōdētes nescio an curioso lectori satis-
fecerint. Vnde obsecro vos o paula et
eustochiū fundatis. p me ad dūm pre-
ces: ut quādiu i hoc corpusculo sū scri-
bā aliqd gratū vobis vtile ecclesie: di-
gnū posteris. Presentiū quiqz iudiciuz
oblatratiū nō satis moueor: qz in vtrā-
qz parte aut amore labunt aut odio.
Explicit plog9 Incipit daniel. ppheta

Anno tercio regni io-
achim regis iuda ve-
nit nabuchodono-
sor rex babilonis ihe-
rusalē et obsedit eā.
Et tradidit domin9
in manu ei9 ioachim regē iude et parte
vasorū domus dei z asportauit ea in
terrā sennaar in domū dei sui: z vasa
intulit in domū thesauri dei sui. Et ait
rex asanez pposito eunuchoz ut intro-
duceret de filijs isrl et de semine regio.
et tyrānorū pueros i quibz nulla esset
macula decoros forma et eruditos o-

disciplina: z qui possent stare in pala-
tio regis: ut doceret eos litteras et lin-
guam chaldeoz. Et cōstituit eis rex an-
nonā per singulos dies de cibis suis
et vino vnde bibebat ipse: ut enutriti
tribz annis postea starent in cōspectu
regis. Fuerūt ergo inter eos de filijs iude daniel ananias misahel et azarias.
Et imposuit eis ppositus eunuchoru
nomina danieli balthazar: ananie
sidrac misaheli misac et azarie abde-
nago. Proposuit aūt daniel in corde
suo ne pollueretur de mēsa regis neqz
de vino potus ei9: z rogauit eunuchoz
ppositū ne cōtaminaret. Dedit aūt deus danieli gratiam et misericordiam
in cōspectu principis eunuchoz. Et
princeps eunuchoz ad daniele. Timeo
ego dūm meū regē qui cōstituit vobis
cibū et potū: qui si viderit vultus vros
maciletiores pre ceteris adolescentibz
coeuis vestris: condemnabitis caput
meū regi. Et dixit daniel ad malasser
quē cōstituerat princeps eunuchoz super danielem ananiā misahelē z aza-
riam. Tempta nos obsecro seruos tuos
diebus dece et dētur nobis legumina
ad vescendū et aqua ad bibendum: z
cōtemplare vultus nostros et vultus
pueroz qui vescuntur cibo regio: et si-
cut videris facies cū seruis tuis. Qui
audito sermone huiuscemodi tempta-
uit eos diebz decem. Post dies aūt decem apparuerūt vultus eoz meliores
et corpulentiores: pre omnibus pueris
qui vescebātur cibo regio. Porro malasser tollebat cibaria et vinū potus
eorum: dabatqz eis legumina. Pueris
aūt hijs dedit deus scientiā et discipli-
nam in omni libro et sapientia: dani-
li aūt intelligentiā omniū visionum

of printing revolutionized the way people thought and reacted to news, gossip, hearsay, lore, and fact. Printing also encouraged more people to write. And as they began to read and write with proficiency, they found they derived profound pleasure from these skills as well.

It can be argued that the pivotal event in the evolution of written communication was the invention of the printing press by the German goldsmith-turned-printer Johannes Gensfleisch, aka Gutenberg (c. 1397-1468). Although movable type in the form of wooden blocks had been invented in China around A.D. 1040 and metal type can be traced to thirteenth-century Korea, in pre-Renaissance Europe, books were mainly copied out by hand. Some books were also printed by woodblock, with words and illustrations sharing the same block. No one other than the clergy and a few learned men could read or write. Virtually no one read or wrote for the sheer pleasure of doing so.

Folio 131 of the Book of Daniel in the Morgan Library's copy of the second volume of the Latin Bible printed by the firm of Gutenberg and Fust (c. 1455) is ornamented not only with an initial cap, but also with delicate handpainted filigree work that wraps the left-hand column of the text.

During the Renaissance, however, with the explosion of learning, the growth of universities and an attendant rise of a literate bourgeoisie, the desire to read spread. Secular scribes, banded together in guilds and fraternities, began to be asked to write out everything from records of transactions to documents to books on a wide range of subjects— and in the vernacular, not just in the Latin penned by their religious counterparts in the monasteries. One noted Italian scribe, Poggio Bracciolini, traveled widely throughout Europe in search of an adaptable letterform that could be penned with greater speed. Based on his observations, two scripts, *corsiva humanista* and *corsiva cancellaresca*, were formulated—but despite his efforts, no scribe could outpace the demand for portable books that could be read by the individual.

Wishing to replicate liturgical manuscripts in quantity without sacrificing the clarity of their original design, Gutenberg came up with the idea of framing lines of interchangeable type within a mold so that multiples of a text could be produced. Utilizing cast-metal letters invented by his friend Peter Schoeffer, Gutenberg formed a partnership in his home city of Mainz with a sponsor, Johann Fust, who financed the invention of his adjustable

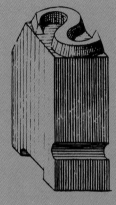

molds, a printing press (modeled on a winepress), and a new, oilier ink. Gutenberg unfortunately squandered so much money on his project—16,000 guilders, or the equivalent of $50,000 today—that Fust deprived him of his patent; Gutenberg died penniless.

The first dated printing issued from Gutenberg's press was a Thirty-One-Line papal indulgence, in 1454. Although he had started working on his most famous work, a 642-page Bible, before the indulgence, the Bible came out later. Known as the Forty-Two-Line Bible for the number of lines set in each column, the Bible, in Latin, mimicked the German Gothic-style script by utilizing 270 different characters, some of which were combined. About 180 copies of the Bible were printed, three copies of which, including one on vellum, reside in the collection of rare books and manuscripts held by the Pierpont Morgan Library in New York City.

At first, printed books on paper—the earliest of them called *incunabula*—were intended only to be less costly alternatives to "real" books, on vellum, which continued to be transcribed by

In the traditional method of printing called letterpress, each individual letter, such as the S pictured here, is set up on a composing stick, with blanks between words as well as between the sticks, or lines of type. The type case OPPOSITE for any font contains multiples of each letter and numeral, with the largest sections reserved for the letters, or "sorts," that are used most frequently. The expression "to be out of sorts" refers to the typesetter running out of a particular letter.

A	B	C	D	E	F	G
H	I	K	L	M	N	O
P	Q	R	S	T	V	X
â	ê	î	ô	û	Y	Z
á		í	ó	ú	;	
à	è	ì	ò	ù		*fl*
*		J	U	j		*ff*

A	B	C	D	E	F	G
H	I	K	L	M	N	O
P	Q	R	S	T	V	X
J	U	Æ	Æ	§	Y	Z
ffl	¶	Œ	Œ	†	[ ]	!
fl	Ç	ç	W	w	( )	?
ff	ë	ï	ü	É	É	"

o   ç   é   ~   ,

& b c d e

z l m n i

y

x v u t   ESPACES

1 2 3 4 5 6 7 8

s f *f* g h   9 o   æ œ

o p q *ffi* ffi k   DEMI QUADRA-LINS

fi fi :   QUADRA-LINS

a r . ,   QUADRATS

calligraphers. Printing, indeed, was not supposed to eradicate a need for scribes, and because of this, the type in many early books mimics calligraphy. By 1501, thousands of printed books were in circulation, covering genres as various as grammar, poetry, history, and even table manners—as well as devotional texts. Some early books relied more on their illustrations than on the text to inform their readers. To the unlearned, the picture served as the most effective tool to get a message across—much as comic books do today to those with limited reading skills.

In 1475, the first book to be printed in English was produced by a British diplomat attached to the Belgian court, William Caxton. Proficient in several languages, Caxton concentrated his energies on translating (from French into English) and printing a history of Troy. Later based in a printing shop near Westminster Abbey, Caxton ultimately printed over one hundred books, many of which had originally appeared in Latin, French, and Dutch. His best known work is an edition of Chaucer's *Canterbury Tales*.

From the early sixteenth century on, virtually every country in Europe enjoyed a huge output in printed matter, much of which was issued in response to and coinciding with periods of religious ferment and political upheaval, as well as spurts of intense intellectual activity, especially in the arena of scientific discovery. Indeed, nothing has changed, except in terms of technological advancement and innovation. People still want to know what is going on in their world, and despite the impact of the Internet and the World Wide Web, people still look primarily to printed matter—and to books—to garner information.

At Kate's Paperie, we employ a number of styles of printing when we are asked to personalize stationery and other specialty papers such as invitations. The shape, size, and texture of paper influence the choice of typography. The edges of the paper can be explored as boundaries to a design, as can the size and style of the lettering.

These days, we find that it usually takes from two to three weeks to process an order for a monogram or other custom-engraved adornment. As the dies for several monograms are prepared at Crane & Co., the engraving artist inspects them through a magnifying glass called a loupe to check for any imperfections, such as burrs along the edges of the letters that would blur the clean lines of the overall composition. Hand-tooling letters corrects these flaws.

The traditional letterpress relief-printing method is practiced in much the same way as it was in Gutenberg's day. Although labor intensive and time consuming, letterpress fosters an enormous sense of accomplishment, both in the professional and in the amateur printer.

Blind embossing, letterpress, and engraving are the three most tactile ways to personalize stationery or other paper goods; you can literally feel the impression each makes, be it raised or recessed. Because they are custom designed and crafted, these forms also appear more formal than the imprints, such as offset lithography or laser printing, that are created by computer. The latter, though, are far more economical, especially if you are expert at computer graphics; with them you can design your own letterhead.

Choosing a typeface and setting the individual letters in their metal bars, locking up the plate, and designing a printed sheet or page are all pleasurable pursuits, as is choosing a receptive paper. Medium-weight and thick rag papers work best because they can withstand the pressure of type as the sheet of paper is hand-fed into the press. As the rollers ink the type, there's a breathless moment of anticipation before witnessing the final result. The pressure of the press may depress (deboss) the type or image into the paper. The tactile appreciation of a letterpress sheet is immediate and highly sensual.

In general, embossing (and its opposite, debossing) are techniques we at Kate's Paperie recommend primarily for the creation of monograms and short forms of address. In embossing, the letters (or image) are cast into a metal or plastic die that creates—or sculpts—a raised impression when it is pressed into the paper. Blind embossing is the same as embossing, but without ink.

Engraving, like letterpress, is an age-old art. Also known as intaglio printing, it is particularly graceful because it emulates calligraphy in its precision and delicacy. Engraving ensures a fine, sharp line. Once executed by hand-tooling letters or images—in their reverse—upon a copper plate or steel die, engraving is now typically accomplished by a less costly process known as photoengraving. Light passing through a photosensitive film coating the engraving plate defines the letters or images. After the

removal of the film, the plate is acid-etched to incise the lettering into its surface. When fed through the press, the paper picks up ink in the cavities created by the engraving; the ink adheres to the raised surface of the letters. The press may create a pressure of upwards of two tons per square inch, so the paper selected must exhibit exceptional tensile strength, especially if it is to be inked in more than one color.

Thermography, which imitates engraving, costs far less because it employs no dies or plates. In a five-step process, special resinous powders are melted, then fused by heat, to the inked letters or images; when the powder heats, it swells, resulting in a raised effect. You can tell the difference between engraving and thermography by inspecting the back of the paper. An engraved die or plate will leave an indentation whereas thermography will not. Thermography inks also appear shinier than those used in engraving.

Most of the printing we do at Kate's Paperie is requested for writing papers or for invitations, especially wedding invitations and their accompanying enclosures. Of all the different forms of stationery, the one that continues to adhere most rigorously to time-honored rules of etiquette is the wedding invitation. The choice of paper, the style of the engraving, the wording of the invitation, and the presentation within the envelope are traditions that have endured virtually unchanged for decades.

The traditional invitation is printed from a custom-engraved copper plate, in one of several formal typefaces, on a double-fold sheet of ivory-toned or ecru medium-weight paper. (In Europe, the paper preference is white.) In our parents' day, the invitation was folded again, but now this custom of an extra fold is rarely invoked. The invitation may request either "the pleasure of your company" or "the honour of your presence." The latter form is used for more religious settings, such as a church or temple; the former, for a wedding taking place at home or in a club, hall, or other public venue.

A number of enclosures (and, by tradition, a leaf of tissue) usually accompany the invitation. These may include a reception card, a card detailing directions to the venue, and a reply card with its own preaddressed envelope. (In the case of a large reception and a small ceremony, the situation is reversed; here the invitation to the reception is accompanied by a ceremony card, which is inserted for the few guests who are invited to the latter event.) The folded invitation, and the enclosures, with a tissue between, are then inserted in a plain envelope that is inscribed with the recipient's name in a fine calligraphic hand. This envelope tucks neatly into a slightly larger envelope for mailing. The custom of the double envelope dates from the era when invitations were hand-delivered. To protect it from soiling en route, an invitation was placed into two envelopes. The outer envelope was removed and discarded upon delivery.

Kate's Paperie is often approached to print professional stationery, the repertoire of letterhead and business cards (and sometimes résumé paper) that visually attest to a business's corporate identity. When we designed and developed our own stationery and the other paper products that bear the Kate's Paperie name, we became acutely conscious of how important a corporate identity is. The initial impression and impact a letterhead and a business card make are critical to a business relationship. They establish a sense of authority and reinforce an awareness of the business's commitment to its product or service.

The so-called letterhead system—the letterhead itself, plus its envelope and a business card (and any other paper products considered relevant to a corporate identity, such as package labels, fax transmittal sheets, invoices, and note cards)—is your proxy; it stands in for you when you are not present in person. Paper and printing join forces to cement your image. Who you are and what you do should be reflected in your choice of both.

For the past century, the standard size and format for stationery used for business correspondence has remained consistent: the so-called English standard 8 ½ inches-by-11 inches single sheet of a medium-weight bond, which is the size that conveniently fed the typewriter. A second type of stationery, in a slightly smaller size—the monarch at 7 ¼-by-10 ½ inches—complements the larger format but tends to be reserved for more personal messages and for cover notes that would accompany a report or other document. (In Europe, the standard letterhead, based on the metric system and known by the term "A4," measures 210-by-297 millimeters.) When you consider a design for your letterhead, it is wise to remember that the design must suit as many types of stationery and ancillary papers as you plan to keep on hand. The letterhead is composed of one's name, title, address, and other relevant information, such as telephone and fax numbers and an E-mail address, if desired. Because of its more personal nature, monarch stationery customarily deletes everything but the name and title. The company name and

Today, more and more people are taking an active role in creating the cards that mark such joyful occasions in their lives as the birth of a child or a wedding. Most want to respect rules of etiquette, but at Kate's Paperie, we encourage them to consider these not as rules but as guidelines. For ecological reasons and to save on costs, for example, we suggest that wedding enclosures not be accompanied by an extra envelope, as these are no longer relevant. We always counsel our customers to be sensitive to the properties of the paper they select; some papers simply beg for letterpress, while others look better engraved.

ANSON & PRATT

MANUFACTURERS OF
"The Anson Patent Plumbers Friend"
OR WASTE PIPE CLEANER.

Plumbing, Hot Water and Steam Heating.

Hastings, Nebraska, _____ 189_

top. Lift out the plunger (2) and
you have a direct use for the
"Anson."

This is the foulest closet used
and unless frequently cleaned with
the Anson is a disease breeder.

Most Respt.
Miller & Dennis.
per F. B.

C. F. Adams Company

Importers, Jobbers and Dealers in
Household Necessities.

Hartford, Conn., Jan. 17, 1905.

Mr. Thos. W. Walker,
41 High St.,
Willimantic, Ct.

Dear Sir:

Your letter of Jan. 16th is received. In reply would
say that commissions are due the agent on each Saturday night
after the first week, that is if you sell a party $10.00 worth
the party pays you 50¢ to start with and signs a lease agreeing
to pay for this $10.00 article at the rate of 25¢ per week, which
amount is called for by another man or collector weekly, and as
soon as this collector sees the party and has agreed to keep the
article and signs a contract to that effect the commission is
due the agent the following Saturday night. The agent is to no
expense except his own personal expense for board, etc., as we
furnish all the stock and the teams, so that your expense is no
more than if you were paying your board in Willimantic. It is
well for an agent to have enough to carry him along for a couple
of weeks until he gets familiar with the business, and if he begins to make sales you can see that he has some cash coming in on
each sale to meet his daily expenses besides the balance which will
be coming to him on the following Saturday night. This business
is like everything else, it is simply a matter of hustle, allowing
that a man has fair ability, and if he will stick to it and follow
instructions there is no question of his being able to make money,
and that just as fast as he can sell the goods. Our business is
thoroughly established all through the state and the line is nothing that people are not familiar with, and the small payments make
it a strong inducement for people to buy in this way.

Hoping you will decide to start in with us, we are

Yours truly,
C. F. Adams Co.

CLYDE BEATTY
TRAINED WILD ANIMAL
CIRCUS

CLYDE BEATTY
Owner

WINTER QUARTERS, FORT LAUDERDALE, FLORIDA

RALPH J. CLAWSON
General Manager

Empire Brush Block Co.

MANUFACTURERS OF
OSTRICH FEATHER DUSTERS
BRUSH BLOCKS AND BRUSH HANDLES

171-173 SUFFOLK STREET

New York, Jan 31 1912

Messrs Reeves & Todd
165 Broadway.
New York City

Gentlemen,—

Your letter of the 29 inst at
hand and have noted contents. We beg to
state that you will have to send this claim
to your New Jersey representative for collection

Very truly Yours
Empire Brush Block Co.
per L. Herrman

Frank Riley 220 East 42nd Street New York

TELEPHONE MOHAWK 4-6300

Printed by letterpress on STRATHMORE BOND, Ivory, Wove, Substance 24

MARK G. GODDARD   J. GILBERT GODDARD

GODDARD TRUNK COMPANY
NEW ORLEANS — LA

This is Uncle Sam Bond, Canary, 17 x 22-28. The use of
a distinctive color for a letterhead serves as a trade
mark. The first essential, however, is to select a paper
in which the color does not vary. Every lot must be
exactly the same shade. The second essential is the
selection of harmonizing colors in the design. This
treatment, printed in three colors, gives a striking
letterhead that is sure to be remembered.

Distributors of Steam Airplane · Lycoming Motors · Smith Controllable Propellers

HARRY R. PLAYFORD INC.
CLEVELAND AIRPORT · CLEVELAND O.

TELEPHONES
FIELD · CLEARWATER 2600
BRANCH · LONGACRE 4750

(This is White Howard Bond Ripple 24 lb. Substance)

PHOENIX DRESS CO.
MAKERS OF DISTINCTIVE DRESSES AND GOWNS

712 NORTH FIFTH ST.
MILWAUKEE, WIS.

(This is White Howard Bond Linen 24 lb. Substance)

LETTERHEAD DESIGNED BY GUSTAV JENSEN FOR WORCESTER SILK MILLS CORPO-
RATION · PRINTED BY THE DAVIDSON PRESS, INC. ON OLD CHESTER MADE BY THE
AMERICAN WRITING PAPER COMPANY · COURTESY MORTON FREUND ADVERTISING

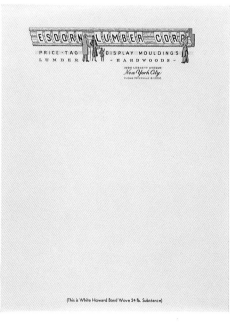

(This is White Howard Bond Wove 24 lb. Substance)

The evolution of a corporate identity and business letterhead reflects the personality of a company—and how that company wishes to be perceived by the public. Most letterheads are designed, for obvious reasons, to be positioned at the top of the sheet of stationery, but from time to time, a corporate identity, such as that of the International Stock Food Company AT LEFT, will spill over the page. These days, manifest explosions of corporate exuberance tend to be held in check, and letterheads, for the most part, are more elegant and restrained. The least costly way to reproduce letterhead for business stationery is by offset or laser printing; many offset printers require a minimum order of 500 sheets. Because many people equate a business image, or seriousness of intent, with a fine-quality paper, the selection of a smooth, attractive paper in a thicker stock will create the look of a more expensive printing technique, even when only computer-based technology is employed.

Atelier

44

DAVID WOLFE
FINE PRINTER

44 Pleasant St.
Portland, Maine 04101
207–772–0811

Atelier   *44*

ERIC BAKER DESIGN ASSOCIATES, INC.

11 EAST 22ND STREET

NEW YORK, NY 10010

TELEPHONE: 212.598.9111

FAX: 212.598.5941

Kate's Paperie

Joseph Barreiro
President

8 West 13th Street
New York, NY 10011
Tel: (212) 633-0570
Fax: (212) 366-6532

561 Broadway
New York, NY 10012
Tel: (212) 941-9816
Fax: (212) 941-0194

A business card typically represents a corporate identity in microcosm, condensing image and information onto a few square inches of paper. Some liberties can be taken with this format, though; for example, both sides can be printed, or the card can be designed to be folded so that it can incorporate additional information. If you examine the cards on this page, you will note how they carry a subliminal message beyond what is printed upon them. For example, we have experimented with a number of formats here at Kate's Paperie; the one featured above exhibits a deckled edge, which represents paper made by hand on a mold. In a simple, straightforward manner, Eric Baker's card underscores how graphic design hews to basic principles of proportion and spacing, while David Wolfe's exhibits his expertise as a printer. Nina Ong's unusual card relays an image of efficiency in a non-traditional format with a subtle sense of wit; her card can also be utilized as a luggage tag or package label.

nina ong
211 thompson street, 3m
new york, ny 10012
212.982.9668
nong@worldnet.att.net

970032

address (and logo, if any) are often placed in the upper-left corner of the sheet, or at the top center, but you do not have to be limited by these options. You can position your letterhead anywhere, as long as it is in a place that is not apt to be covered by what is to be written on the page.

Once the design of the letterhead is established, you must select a paper. In the 1920s, the colors considered most tasteful for business stationery papers were white and dove gray, although cream and a slightly darker beige were also acceptable. In most cases, the same holds true today. Ink was, by tradition, black. Black is still the norm, but another color may be used if you believe it will project your image in a more convincing manner.

Finally, be sure to consider how the business stationery is likely to be used in the office. The paper you choose should be compatible with your photocopier and computer printer so that whatever you print on the stationery will not look discordant with the letterhead.

Business cards are an indispensable part of the professional stationery repertoire. A business card, too, should make a good first impression, especially as it may be kept on file and consulted again and again by its recipient. Although most American business cards measure 3½-by-2 inches, this format is by no means a size you must adhere to. In fact, cards used by multinational corporations conform to a larger, credit-card format. The only guidelines are ones of convenience: how will you carry your cards and how and where do you plan to store them? Card stock should be heavy and strong, especially if it is to be folded. Book folds, gate folds, tent folds, and *Z* folds are options that are being selected more and more; the extra space offered by the fold format allows for more information—such as a second address or a re-peat of all information in a second language—to be printed on the card.

Not a day goes by without a note that must be written, a message sent, a transaction conducted by letter. Virtually every formality of our lives is documented by some form of written text. Oftentimes that text—be it a contract, a letter of agreement or intent, or some other form—is accompanied by correspondence, which serves as testament and validation. Informal correspondence is an important part of our everyday lives, too. Whether we communicate by postcard, greeting card, note card, or chit, or by E-mail or facsimile, we want to get our message across to our friends and loved ones. We want to stay in touch.

As soon as a child learns to write, the art of correspondence begins. From an endearingly scrawled "I love you Mom and Dad" penciled on a Valentine heart to a more formalized "Thanks for the present" to a grandma on the occasion of a birthday, we instill in our children the idea that a heartfelt message is properly expressed on paper. In an age when computer technology engages us more and more, we are reminded that the handwritten letter remains the most polite and appropriate form of communication in many situations. Indeed, many situations require it. It would be considered rude to E-mail a note of condolence, for instance, just as it would be to type out a thank-you in response to a gift.

Throughout history, letters have been the major means of communicating what was really happening in the world, and not what might be filtered through censors or editors. Because they are, for the most part, spontaneous, immediate, and unaffected, letters offer an intimate glimpse into everyday life as well as an unguarded commentary on world-shaking events. In ancient Europe, most missives involved legal transactions, but social communications were not unheard of. An invitation thought to have been written in the third century A.D. reads:

"Eudaemon invites you
to dine at the Gymnasium
in celebration of the crowning
of his son on the first at the
eighth hour."

The Romans enjoyed sending one another personal notes. They also utilized lengthy instructional apistles to get a message across to a large audience. Great thinkers such as Horace and the apostles of the early Christian church adopted the epistle as a forum to communicate what they thought and believed because they could be rapidly assimilated by the listener.

In the Middle Ages, writing a letter was considered a more strenuous feat than fighting a battle. Virtually everyone, except a handful of clergy and learned men, was illiterate; feudal lords and courtiers were able to identify themselves only with a slash or other such mark. Knights realized that to distinguish friend from foe when fully suited up in armor, they required a highly visible form of identification. To this end, they developed

Many contemporary cards and papers are so joyful in spirit that they tempt adults and children alike into keeping up with faraway family and friends. When a message is dear—or a card is too pretty to throw away—it is fun to showcase it on a ribbon board. Cut a board in a convenient size, paint it or cover it with fabric, and crisscross ribbons over its surface. Secure the ribbons with thumbtacks to hold cards in place.

The Greeks practiced a form of writing called boustrophedon, whereby words ran from right to left and back again "like an ox turning in" a field. Similarly, in the nineteenth century, many correspondents wrote letters in perpendicular directions—and saved on paper costs in the process. Writing like this, in the style called double-crossing or in code, was one way to ensure a modicum of privacy, too, especially if the letter was of an intimate nature.

coats of arms—*cote d'armes*—to slip over their suits of mail. These emblems were affixed to other objects, such as banners and chimneypieces, as well as to writing papers. In the last case, the coat of arms was converted to a crest; accompanying the crest was a motto derived from a knight's battle cry, which was typically printed on an image of a ribbon unfurled beneath the crest. Crests were hallmarks of class and individuality. It was considered extremely unfit for a lady to use her husband's crest on her own writing paper; no lady had a right to a crest. Over time, that restriction was lifted, first by creating a new crest segmenting the emblem in quarters to identify her as her husband's wife, later by allowing her to adapt the crest to indicate her position within his family.

The eighteenth century is known as the golden age of letters. Memorable troves of correspondence survive from that era, including the 1,500 letters written by Madame de Sévigné to her two daughters that are considered a monument of French literature. Letter writing was also exceedingly popular throughout the nineteenth century and on into our own.

Despite the popularity of writing letters, stationery as we know it was unknown as late as the mid-nineteenth century. To answer a billet-doux, or love note, for example, a lady was obliged to trim a snip off a larger sheet of paper. The so-called trousseau of fine stationery is a Victorian innovation made possible by the Industrial Revolution and the ascendancy of the machine. The Victorians, notorious for governing every aspect of their lives according to the most arcane rules of etiquette, evolved a voluminous inventory of writing papers, which would be used at different times for different occasions. By the turn of the twentieth century, a proper trousseau included, among other items, ladies', gentlemens', and children's visiting cards, mourning cards, ladies' correspondence paper, and gentlemen's club paper. The minimal polite trousseau contained three types of stationery: a flat sheet used by the man of the family, folded sheets used by the lady of the house, and a "superior" paper for "state occasions." To these three might be added smaller, folded notes called informals, plus visiting cards. The monogram, family crest, or address was always engraved at the upper left-hand corner of the household stationery. A man's stationery did not require a fancy monogram, only his initials printed in block letters. Because the day's date distracted from a monogram or address header, the

"TO BE A REALLY GOOD CORRESPONDENT IS TRULY AN ART, PERHAPS FIRST OF ALL A GIFT, TO BE CULTIVATED AND DEVELOPED."

—THE ETIQUETTE OF LETTER WRITING (EATON, CRANE & PIKE, 1927)

writer was expected to record it in the lower left-hand corner of the final page of correspondence, after his or her signature. The date was never abbreviated.

Country and city stationery differed in tone. Informal home papers displayed more playful or amusing color combinations—a red ink on gray paper with a matching red envelope liner, for example— as well as custom-made monograms in idiosyncratic and distinctive designs, and insignia denoting one's hobby or country affiliation, such as yacht club flags or miniature views of one's country house.

It was only a matter of time before the playing card and the visiting card, both of which were highly popular during the eighteenth century, evolved into the postcard and greeting card familiar to us today. The first step was to engrave or print the front of a visiting card with an image, such as an ancient ruin. Later, decorated cards were used to convey "compliments of the season"; the custom was to leave a card behind when making calls to friends on New Year's Day. By the mid-nineteenth century, cards were being produced on a prodigious scale to mark almost any occasion you could think of—as they continue to be today.

Prior to World War II, the choreography of writing a letter on a piece of folded stationery with a fountain pen was dictated by the size of the blotter. Two methods were prescribed by etiquette books. The most common sequence was to begin on the front page, flip to the last, then back to the third, and then the second. The front to the second progression traveled from the back page to the second and lastly the third if the blotter was large enough to blot these two pages simultaneously. Intimate letters were penned only on the second and third pages, to conceal words from view.

Even though the decades following World War II have witnessed a simplifying of forms of address and types of formal stationery, the variety of types of informal stationery, postcards, greeting cards, and the like has increased greatly.

If brevity is the soul of wit, then the postcard and greeting card are the ideal formats for writing messages that are short and sweet, if not funny. Since 1869, when the postcard was first introduced in Austria as a carefree alternative to formal stationery, the postcard has been an omnipresent means of communication. When you want to let someone know you're thinking of them in just a few words, there's nothing quite like a postcard.

The postcard gets its message across in two ways, by the picture on its face and by the message inscribed by the writer on its reverse side. Since the innovation of the picture postcard by the French as a touristic device to entice visitors to the just-erected Eiffel Tower, the postcard has excelled as a merchandising tool. In America, hundreds of millions of postcards were purchased and sent between 1898 and the onset of the First World War.

Postcard 1

Feb. 1. 1923
N. Bridgton N.H.

THIS SIDE FOR CORRESPONDENCE.

FEB 23 1923

Dear Cousin Mary —

a few lines to let
you know that we
are all well and
hope these few lines
will find you the
same. I can't say
much on this card
but will write
you a long letter soon.
take good care of your
self.
Cousin Mary Comeau

THE ADDRESS TO BE WRITTEN
ON THIS SIDE.

Miss Mary Calquhoun
Ward BB
Davers State
Hospital
Hawthorne,
Mass.

U.S. POSTAGE
1 CENT

PRINTED IN GERMANY

Postcard 2

VICKSBURG
DEC

THIS SPACE FOR CORRESPONDENCE

Dear Grand pa. How are you?
Your Baby says she just loves and
can hardly wait for Uncle Charley
And I just think I had a card from
her and she said he would bring
me a lot of things if I write you.
He good and I am writing you
hard to be good. I want you
would be here. hug and kiss the
candy accept the Best Love to the
everyone from Your Baby
Loves to
all and a Love.

THIS SPACE FOR ADDRESS ONLY

Mr. S. L. Chandler,
Tropico
Cal.
Box #36.

U.S. POSTAGE
ONE CENT

Although greeting cards have been around for centuries—even the ancient Egyptians sent greetings on sheets of papyrus—it was only with the mass-marketing of this mode of communication by J. C. Hall, founder of Hallmark Cards in Kansas City, that greeting cards evolved into the near-universal medium of sending good wishes we know today. To Hall, a "card with a sentiment enclosed" was the perfect vehicle for people who tended to be shy about expressing their feelings. Everyday cards, friendship cards, and congratulatory cards honoring special occasions such as birthdays, weddings, and anniversaries were soon joined by seasonal greetings. One card, entitled "My Friend" and written by a popular newspaper columnist, Edgar Guest, remained in the Hallmark lineup for over fifty years. Today, over one-half of all personal correspondence in the United States is conducted by greeting card, with the preponderance sent at Christmas, Valentine's Day, and Mother's Day.

Today, too, the postcard is making a comeback, both as a collectible and as an avant-garde means of transmitting a commercial message. For the collector, the hundreds of thousands of subjects depicted on antique postcards can be loosely categorized both by period and by type; view cards, displaying all sorts of sites from tourist attractions to scenes of small-town life, are especially sought after. Contemporary subjects for postcards range from the the sublime to the sensational. Postcard books compiling mini-collections of a famous artist's oeuvre, for example, are readily available, as are freebie postcards, often racked in a conspicuous spot in coffee bars and other high-traffic locations, which tout the latest pop recording or fashion statement.

Postcards and greeting cards are enjoyable to make at home as well. With thick card stock and the decorative possibilities afforded by paints, inks, stickers, and rubber stamps—as well as the photocopier and computer—you can send a loved one or a friend a truly personal token of your affection.

Until the middle of the nineteenth century, most letters were folded and sealed with wax. The postmaster wrote the cost of the postage on the side of the letter displaying the address, and then hand-canceled the amount of that postage with a rubber stamp. The tradition of the seal dates back to the earliest days of human communication, when potters stamped seals into clay as marks of identification. In Roman times, epistles were incised on waxed tablets known as *pugillares*, which were connected by a

The invention of the penny postcard—or "postal"—ushered in a new, abbreviated form of correspondence, which was convenient for people who preferred to lean on that old adage "A picture is worth a thousand words." The message that can be contained on a postcard must be distilled to a few, quick impressions or salient facts accompanied by greetings and good wishes. Because it can be read by anyone, a postcard is typically more casual in tone, too. In the era when mail was delivered several times a day, the phrase "Drop me a line" was taken seriously; with speedy deliveries, a card might garner a response within hours.

string fastened by a wax seal, a concept that gave birth, it is believed, to the expression "break open a letter." Waxed tablets were bulky and inconvenient to carry, though, and so eventually were supplanted by parchment scrolls. A scroll could be rolled, sealed with wax, and carried as easily as a quiver of arrows. Monarchs and heads of state used wax seals to authenticate important documents. Medieval seals were often embossed on both sides, with the title of the official on one side. Simplified forms of seals evolved into monograms. Wax was a perfect medium for securing a letter as it could be heated, impressed, and affixed rapidly; wax also hardened almost instantly.

Until the postal service replaced hand delivery of letters, etiquette books decried seals. Sealing the envelope of a letter carried by hand implied that the writer harbored a distrust of the bearer of the letter; instead, the flap of the envelope was to be slid inside. No well-bred person, etiquette decreed, would ever open and read a letter that he or she had been entrusted with. Today, seals and sealing wax are back in style. Waxes come in all sorts of colors. You can find a seal for every letter of the alphabet. Seals can also be custom ordered, much as dies are for custom-engraved letterhead.

Writing a letter is enhanced by the choice of a writing instrument. Words seem to be guided by the flow of pen and ink. Scrawl a message with a pencil; write with care using a fountain pen. The act of refilling the pen inspires reflection; it gives you time to compose your thoughts and, perhaps, rein in maverick feelings.

Two major concerns dictated the evolution of the pen: the nib and the ink supply, both of which affected a pen's speed and accuracy. The goose quills that prevailed from medieval days were finally abandoned in the mid-nineteenth century when the invention of the steel-nibbed pen eliminated the hassle of constantly having to recut a nib. Steel nibs,

Hand-blown glass dip pens from France are grooved so that they will hold enough ink to write one complete standard-size page. With such pens, handmade ink, and sealing wax, you can emulate author Harriet Doerr, who wrote: "I have everything I need . . . a page, a pen, and memory raining down on me in sleeves."

though, were stiff and scratchy. Gold, by contrast, was flexible, if soft. The discovery of a series of metals, such as iridium, that could be fused to gold to lend it strength revolutionized the manufacture of the nib.

Even though a reservoir was built into the structure of the pen from early on, it still had to be filled. Until the late nineteenth century, this was accomplished with an eyedropperlike device called a pipette. Pens often leaked or spit bubbles of ink. To correct the fault, the ink reservoir had to maintain an

"THE LETTER WHICH IS A JOYOUS THING, BRINGING WITH IT
OF A PERSONAL CHAT, IS THE ONE WE SEEK AT THE POS
VOID OF RAMBLING SENTENCES WHICH REQUIRE DISSECTING
BRINGING THE SENDER QUICKLY TO THE MIND'S EYE,

even air pressure. Various devices for drawing ink into the pen were tried, such as the plunger, the snorkel, the pump, the lever, and the syringe. John Jacob Parker's piston mechanism of 1832 and L. E. Waterman's patented capillary-action-channeled "feed" of 1884 are among the innovations that allow today's fountain pens to be self-filling and virtually blot free.

Like watches or fine jewelry, the fountain pen is considered an object of desire, a status object to own and display like any heirloom. Collectible pens made from the 1920s on in hard rubber, celluloid, and casein are in great demand; some are embellished with repoussé or filigree in silver and gold. The best nibs are gold. Today, pens by Parker and Waterman, as well as Cartier, Hakase, Lamy, and Montblanc, and other companies, preserve the tradition of their forerunners. They are beautiful to handle and delightful to behold.

Quill-feather pen nibs were cut according to a rigorous set of specifications. The shape of the nib not only affected how a penman held his pen and sat at his paper, but it also influenced the shape and character of the actual letters. Some letters, for example, had to be created with a nib cut on a slant, while others could be rendered by a pen cut straight across or sliced to a tight point. The depth of the cut also dictated how much ink could be held within the hollow core of the quill. Most penmen had to dip their pens dozens of times to complete even a page of text or a basic letter.

Because so many styles and nibs are available, it is wise to take time to understand the heft and feel of any pen you admire. Test pens if you can. What width nib would you prefer? Do you want the nib to be firm, or would you rather it be fairly flexible? The terms "fine," "medium," and "broad" describe only familiar categories; you will also encounter a choice of styles, such as italic, with its chiseled edge, and oblique, a nib that is cut at a fifteen-degree angle. Pen nibs are also cut to suit the right or left hand. Which would best suit your handwriting?

The earliest inks, made in China, were mixed from soot or lampblack, which was caught and retrieved from a metal cone suspended over a lighted wick. Once the interior of the cone was completely coated in the lampblack, the material was scraped off and mixed with resin and water. The ink was formed into a block or stick, and when needed, some of the ink was mixed in a saucer with a little water.

The main concerns regarding any type of ink have always been how it flows and whether it blots

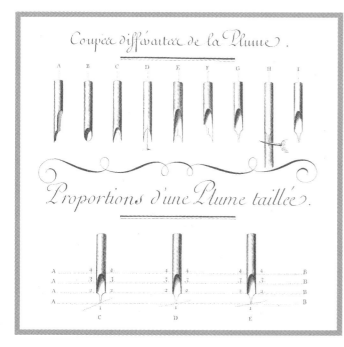

Coupes differantes de la Plume.

Proportions d'une Plume taillée.

or smudges. Although it tended to clog the nib, lampblack was still used late into the Middle Ages, when a slightly more free-flowing ink began to be mixed from crushed oak galls, ferrous sulfate or iron filings, and gums (used as binding agents). When steel nibs were introduced, iron-gall ink proved problematic; it corroded steel.

Experimenting with inks went hand in hand with the development of the pen. Hundreds of formulas were tried over the years but, just as no one universal pen replaced all others, so no universal ink was ever formulated. Most pen manufacturers make inks to be compatible with their own line of pens.

Stationery can be playful or serious, traditional or avant-garde, plain or wildly colorful. No matter what you want to communicate, you will find a paper and envelope to match your every mood and nuance of tone. In our grandparents' era, correspondence was guided by strict forms of etiquette. These days, although certain rules apply—especially with respect to business matters and special occasions such as weddings—you can follow your instinct and let your imagination take flight. Thousands upon

thousands of papers await your pen—
or computer. The possibilities are endless.
Take advantage of them. Writing a letter
or a note can be the most satisfying
endeavor in the world.

That first impression made by a letter is usually conveyed by the paper selected for the letter. How the paper looks and feels transmits a message that can be as strong as that communicated by the words on the sheet. Photocopy paper, appropriate for bulk mailings, would never suit a private or intimate message—but colored stock such as the Rössler line shown here, which is compatible with a laser printer, might overcome that prejudice, especially if the typeface you choose matches the intentions of the message.

It is no wonder that the words "identity" and "image" are used to describe letterhead. Your writing paper says a great deal about who you are. Your choice of paper conveys a subliminal message about your taste and style. Color, texture, and size all speak volumes about how you wish to present yourself to the world.

Paper has always been governed by the size of the mold in which it is formed and/or the press upon which it is printed. But size also has been an indicator of status and social standing. Business letterhead, for example, originally was devised in a large format because it befitted a male-dominated world, while social stationery for women was tailored to be more diminutive and genteel. Most writing paper today is thankfully genderfree, but the types of correspondence that initially suited to a particular sized sheet still do. Business transactions continue to be relayed on bond-size sheets, while thank-yous and other short messages are penned on smaller, fold-over notes and cards.

Today, too, many of the strictest forms of address that dictated how a letter was to be structured have been expunged in favor of a more relaxed attitude toward presentation, especially in terms of opening and closing gambits. No longer must a letter conclude, "I am yours very faithfully," for example; nor must a married woman write out her name in full followed by her husband's full name in parentheses in formal situations. Her own name suffices.

Certain types of stationery that were once used with great frequency, like the mourning card, are rarely seen. Others, though, such as invitation cards, place cards, birth announcements, and even visiting cards, still endear themselves to us and have never gone out of style.

Elegant papers such as those crafted by the Parisian stationer G. Lalo accent a wardrobe beautifully.

As mentioned in the previous chapter, even the most mimimal stationery wardrobe always included large letterhead as well as small fold-over notes. The same is true today. You need a formal paper to write letters on and a less formal paper for notes. If you work from home, your business-related correspondence should follow standard guidelines: 8½-by-11 inch letterhead for formal communications and monarch size, 7¼-by-10 inch sheets for business letters of a more personal nature. Both of these sheets fold into thirds to tuck into their corresponding envelopes. Two other types of writing papers long equated with house stationery are the letter sheet, which folds along the left to double the area for writing, and the so-called half sheet, which measures one-half the size of a formal sheet. Both fold in half to fit their envelopes.

While business and house letterhead feature the name and address, fold-over notes are printed or engraved with the name only, or a monogram or single initial. House letterhead may run your address without your name. Rules applying to the correct exposition of a name are less strict than they used to be. Although it may be considered for a woman to use her "proper social name preceded by her title" on formal stationery, it is no longer mandatory that she

"FASHIONS IN STATIONERY RISE AND FALL, DIFFER AND TURN AS DO THE CURVES IN MILADY'S HAT BRIM."

–JEAN WILDE CLARK
SOCIAL STATIONERY
(EATON, CRANE & PIKE, 1910)

Making a selection of papers for a stationery wardrobe is much the same as assembling a wine cellar. You may follow guidelines set forth in manuals or in books such as this one, but what it all boils down to in the end is a deep inner conviction about what is best for you. An employee who has long overseen our printing division sums it up nicely: "Good is good!" A stationery wardrobe may include plain bond paper used for scribbling, typing, or word processing, and business letterhead and social stationery that is custom designed and printed to your specifications, plus boxed stationery to use when you feel an imprinted paper is unnecessary.

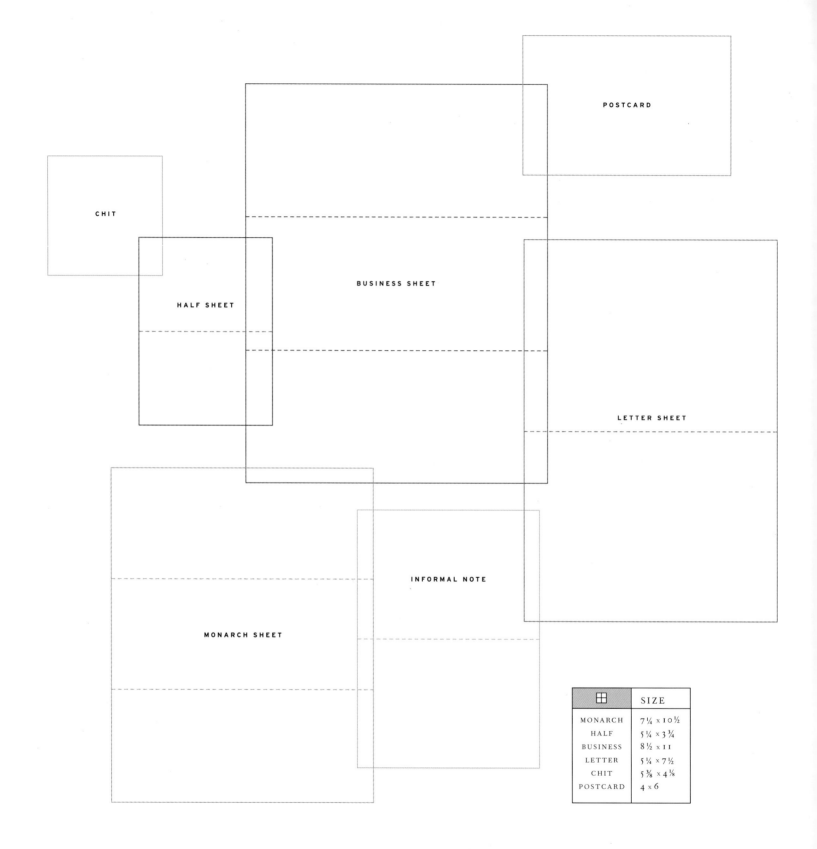

POSTCARD

CHIT

HALF SHEET

BUSINESS SHEET

LETTER SHEET

MONARCH SHEET

INFORMAL NOTE

⊞	SIZE
MONARCH	7 ¼ x 10 ½
HALF	5 ¼ x 3 ¾
BUSINESS	8 ½ x 11
LETTER	5 ¼ x 7 ½
CHIT	5 ⅜ x 4 ⅛
POSTCARD	4 x 6

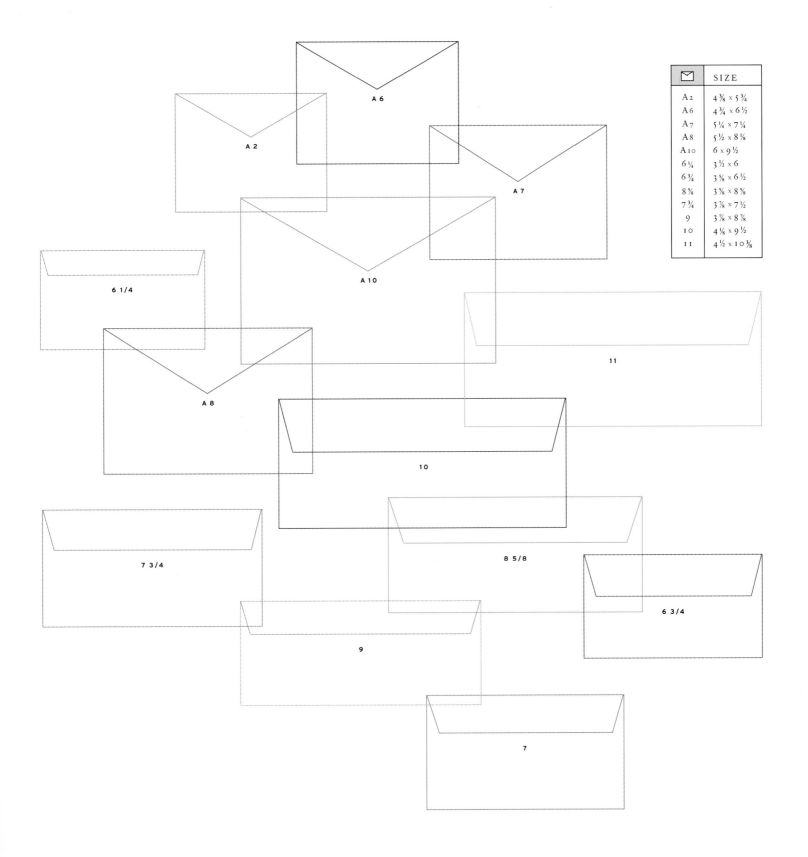

✉	SIZE
A2	4 ⅜ × 5 ¾
A6	4 ¾ × 6 ½
A7	5 ¼ × 7 ¼
A8	5 ½ × 8 ⅛
A10	6 × 9 ½
6 ¼	3 ½ × 6
6 ¾	3 ⅝ × 6 ½
8 ⅝	3 ⅝ × 8 ⅝
7 ¾	3 ⅞ × 7 ½
9	3 ⅞ × 8 ⅞
10	4 ⅛ × 9 ½
11	4 ½ × 10 ⅜

A 6

A 2

A 7

A 10

6 1/4

11

A 8

10

7 3/4

8 5/8

6 3/4

9

7

do so. When in doubt, use a monogram or an initial. If you are inclined to follow codes of etiquette, none of the above papers should be written on the back. Instead, you should continue your correspondence on a compatible second sheet, and you should try to complete your note inside the fold, or move to a paper in a larger format.

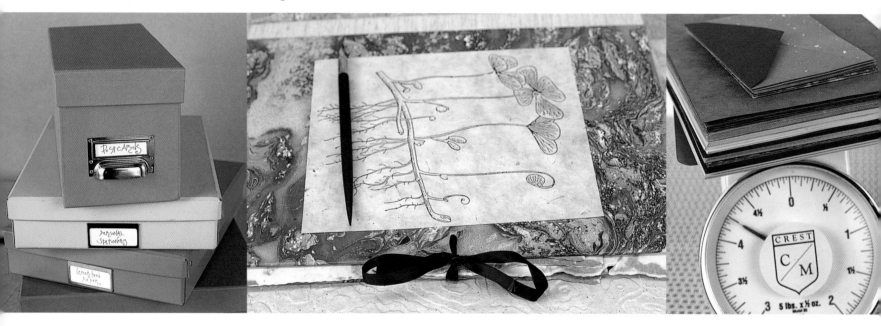

When stationery is treated wisely and with respect, it will serve you well. Proper maintenance of your papers is imperative, but methods of storage may be fun and creative. Kate's Paperie carries all sorts of decorative boxes, envelopes, and portfolios to give people ideas about how to organize their desks at home or in the office. Boxes made from colorful recycled board are one solution; choose boxes that follow the measurements of your cards, sheets, and envelopes as closely as possible. Angela Ligouri's beribboned, marbled portfolios enclose individual writings and drawings like the covers of a book. Paper by the pound can be divvied up into portfolios, too, such as these made from recycled corrugated paper and woven raffia.

Paper size has long been important, it seems, to image. According to an exhaustive description by Pliny the Elder in his *Natural History*, the Romans devised a method of ranking and classifying papyrus sheets based on their size and quality. Whiteness was judged, as was porosity. At first, the finest sheets were classified as *Hieratica*—these measured 11 fingers or digits (8 inches) in width and were reserved for sacred topics. But when Augustus became emperor, the highest classification was renamed for him: *Augustae*. *Augustae* described a new, wider, 13-digit (9½-inch-wide) sheet. With the second-best papyrus, *Charta Livia*, named for his wife, *Hieratica* slipped to third place. Lowest on the scale was a 6 digit (4⅜-inch-wide) papyrus called *Emporetica*, which was used by shop owners to wrap their wares.

Many papers still bear disarmingly fanciful names that allude to their size and purpose. The aptly named atlas, for instance, signifies paper used for maps. Billet note, measuring 6 by 8 inches and charmingly translated as "billet-doux"—literally, "sweet note"—was the paper of choice for abbreviated messages of affection. Foolscap is one of many early papers taken from an ancient watermark,

in this case one depicting a court jester. Foolscap actually comes in two sizes; the version targeted for writing is one-half-inch shorter and one-quarter-inch narrower than the version used for printing purposes. Originally marked with an elephant, the robust (23 by 28 inches) paper of the same name was developed for plate printing as well as drawing.

Early, primitive visiting cards— what we term calling cards—were fashioned by trimming off the edges of playing cards that were all the rage during the eighteenth century. At that time, many invita-

Color coding will cue you in to the contents of each portfolio. A stiffened pouch like the one above, which is folded from dyed goatskin parchment, will showcase custom papers such as those TOP RIGHT made by Studio Z Mendocino, decorated with letterpress designs.

tions for dinners and balls (called tickets) were also circulated on playing cards. Visiting cards assumed such stature that celebrated artists of the day were commissioned to design them. During the Victorian era, colorful embellishments were eliminated in favor of the formal name of the bearer of the card. As with all their social customs, the Victorians developed an arcane hierarchy regarding the size of visiting cards; a strict etiquette also governed how these cards were to be engraved and presented. Only certain typefaces were tolerated. Initially, the engraving had to be executed in a script face, but later this was modified to include a few formal roman-style faces. Until she came out in society, a young woman was not allowed to have a card of her own. In her first season, as a debutante, she shared a card with her mother. This shared card, was smaller in size than her mother's personal card and her mother's name took top billing over her own. According to Crane & Co., the size of a visiting card is still dictated by gender and status in the family and in society. A child's card, logically, is the smallest—2 ¼-by-1 ⅜ inches—while a married couple's is the largest, at 3 ⅜-by-2 ½ inches. A single woman may carry a card measuring 2 ⅞-by-2 inches, while her married counterpart is entitled to a 3 ⅛-by-2 ¼ inch card. A man has a choice: 3 ⅜-by-1 ½ inches or 3 ½-by-2 inches. These days, calling cards are most often used as gift enclosures; they are a handsome way to announce your congratulations and good wishes.

With the passing of such entertainments as formal musicales and private theatricals, few pre-engraved cards requesting "a favor of a reply" remain in the repertoire of social stationery. No longer are women expected to be "At Home" one day a week, nor does anyone require a set of cards listing the times of arrival of the closest train for a house party. Still, preengraved cards are handy for invitations to a formal dinner because most of the necessary information is already printed or engraved upon the card: that the hosts (your names) request the pleasure of———company at——— ———on———at———o'clock, with the address following and, perhaps, a request for an *r.s.v.p.*

In any stationery wardrobe, it is the envelope that makes the first impression. Envelopes convey a sense of mystery and anticipation; some, like the cheerful red ones that signify Valentine's Day, literally make the heart beat faster. The envelope became necessary only when missives grew longer than the single sheet allowed by the penny post. Prior to that time, envelopes were used exclusively by the elite, for special occasions only. The first envelope on record designed to enclose a letter is an autograph letter of 1706 penned by Louis XIV, the Sun King of France. For over a century, it was the French alone who perpetuated the refined novelty of wrapping a letter—*envelopper* is the French term for "to wrap." Mme. de Pompadour, for one, "wrapped" her billets-doux in envelopes delicately scrolled with flowers and leaves.

Once they were introduced to a general public, envelope papers were accompanied by a cardbord template that instructed the user how to shape and fold the envelope before sealing. Lining an envelope was an early-twentieth century development. Borrowing from the new, thin-skinned envelopes used for air-mail letters, producers of envelopes began to make thick, opaque liner envelopes that fit inside slightly larger envelopes to conceal the writing on the letter paper.

The envelope is a triumph of engineering. When unfolded, an envelope resembles nothing so much as a paper airplane, but once doubled over on itself, it forms a tight, taut container that can submit to extensive handling as it makes its way to its destination. These days, envelopes can be divided into two categories: those that will be stuffed by hand and those that are filled by automatic insertion equipment.

Envelopes come in dozens of sizes as well as a variety of shapes. Like a box spring and mattress, the pairing of paper with a complementary envelope ensures a sense of harmony. The paper should tuck neatly within the envelope.

An individual visiting card can be written out in a fine hand, especially when it is used for another purpose altogether, such as a gift en-closure or a place card at table. Boxes of blank gilt-edged cards, therefore, are perfect for spontaneous gestures, as are boxed sets of miscellaneous stationery, which can be used at whim. An extra box of stationery is handy for guests, too.

Some envelopes call for a particular fold; the commonplace #10, for example, takes a standard 8½-by-11-inch sheet folded in three.

Even if it has been made under ideal conditions, is acidfree, and has been treated to withstand deterioration, paper, like any natural material, will age over time. Environmental factors must be taken into consideration, including climate, temperature, light, and moisture. A temperature of between sixty and sixty-five degrees and a relative humidity of between 30 and 70 percent (optimum is 60 percent) are preferred. Prolonged exposure to the air will cause paper to yellow, as will direct sunlight and the ultraviolet rays in fluorescent light. Light and heat can darken paper as well, and will turn it brittle. Light fades inks and colors, and dampness encourages mold to form, as well as the rust-colored mildew spots known as foxing. Dampness will also provoke warping and curling at the edges, while drying can tighten edges causing the center of the sheet to look swollen and distorted. The number one rule of thumb regarding the storage of paper is to lay it

flat. Do not roll it. Cover the paper to keep out dust, and store it in a cool, dry, well-ventilated place away from direct sunlight, moisture, or heat. If you buy sheet paper in quantity, keep it wrapped until you want to use it.

Storing your writing papers is important to their preservation. Because it is an organic material, paper can be affected by damp and by prolonged exposure to sun and heat. Manufacturers design boxed stationery with the intent that it stay in its box, but you may want to keep some sheets, notes, and envelopes in cubbyholes in your desk or in an upright letter holder so that you can access them easily. Metal boxes are recommended for the storage of precious objects because they are fireproof, but metal does not serve paper well. Paper must "breathe"; both metal and plastic will suffocate paper and, if the environment is damp and humid, can trap condensation within the box, which can hasten the onset of mold. Wooden boxes and acid-free cardboard boxes, by contrast, do breathe and can be trusted to stabilize environmental conditions.

People pack Kate's Paperie on Valentine's Day. Everyone wants to find or make just the right card, which is not surprising, given the long history of epistolary romance. Writing how you feel to someone, of course, is an activity that need not be confined to February 14. You can write a love letter anytime, anywhere. Because a love letter is the most thrilling and the most passionate of all forms of letterwriting, your choice of paper should reinforce how you feel. A love letter is for keeps.

SOME AMOROUS
CORRESPONDENTS

THOMAS WOODROW WILSON AND ELLEN AXSON WILSON

LORD ADMIRAL NELSON AND LADY EMMA HAMILTON

SIMONE DE BEAUVOIR AND JEAN-PAUL SARTRE

NATHANIEL AND SOPHIA PEABODY HAWTHORNE

ROBERT AND ELIZABETH BARRETT BROWNING

EDITH WHARTON TO W. MORTON FULLERTON

OSCAR WILDE TO LORD ALFRED DOUGLAS

GEORGE SAND AND ALFRED DE MUSSET

DYLAN THOMAS TO CAITLIN THOMAS

WILLIAM AND MARY WORDSWORTH

JOHN KEATS TO FANNY BRAWNE

NAPOLEON TO JOSEPHINE

Of all containers of the written or printed word, none is as seductive as a book. When you lift a brand-new book off the shelf, crack its spine, and riffle its pages, its whisper is both alluring and reassuring. The smell of the ink on the paper and the texture of the paper itself excite the senses and awaken one's curiosity to the tantalizing unknown harbored therein. A dearly familiar book is, perhaps, the most beloved of any object we might possess. Ask any child. Children love to be read the same story over and over. This love of

"We use books like mirrors, gazing into them only to discover ourselves," wrote Joseph Epstein. Of all the forms a book might take to read us along the journey of life, the journal is the most private and intimate. Jottings, or musings, and spurts of free association all contribute to self-revelation.

storytelling is innate. And why not? Storytelling is an oral tradition that goes back millennia. Today, doomsayers predict the demise of books, but we see no sign of that. People seem to crave books. And journals. At Kate's Paperie we can never keep enough journals in stock. More and more, people are transcribing and describing the stories of their own lives. Reading and writing are here to stay.

Unlike most stationery, which is discarded once it is written on, sent, and read by its recipient, a book has to function as a more or less permanent object, capable of being used—or perused—over and over again. Because a book is typically saved, its leaves must be held together and protected. The binding of the book, including its endpapers and a casing formed by two covers and a connecting spine (and in the case of many hardcover books, a dust jacket) guards the pages against wear, moisture, and decay.

In an old-time bindery, the task of stitching together the signatures that form a book fell to women, while heavier tasks such as pressing just-bound volumes to prevent warping were handled by men. Nontraditional bindings OPPOSITE assume myriad forms, including accordion folds.

VENETIAN BLIND / FOLD BOOK

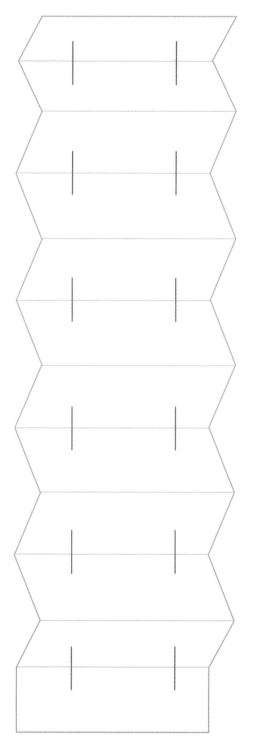

FOLD / CODEX-ATTACHED AT PEAKS

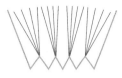

CODEX / FOLD / CODEX

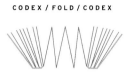

DOS-à-DOS

SOME UNCOMMON
BINDINGS

FOLD / CODEX: ATTACHED AT VALLEYS

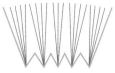

DOS-à-DOS-à-DOS: THE WEDDING CAKE BOOK

FAN / FOLD / FAN

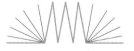

SIX VOLUME CODEX WITH SEPARATE INDEX

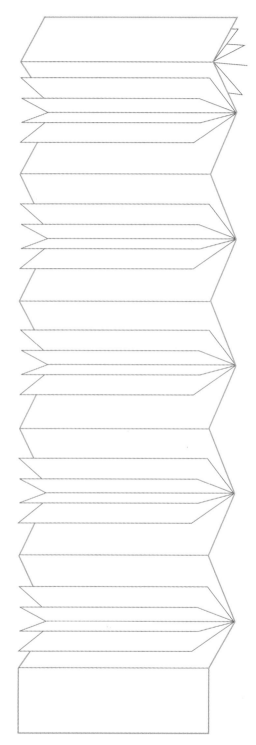

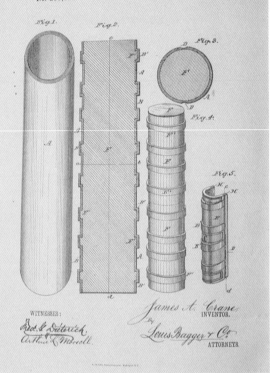

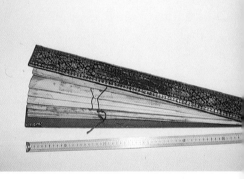

Because a book's casing is made independently of its pages, various timesaving techniques for its manufacture have been attempted over the years. Crane & Co., for example, took out the patent above for the formation of a book spine in 1884.

The earliest books were simply strips of palm or bark with writing scratched or inked upon the surface. The strips fanned out from the cord that tied them together. A pair of battens attached at top and bottom functioned as primitive covers. Later books were written in a more portable and lightweight format, the scroll; it is said the famous library at Alexandria, Egypt, housed half a million works in this format.

During the time of the Romans and in early Europe prior to printing, books returned to a multileaf format, which was called by the term "codex." The way the parchment was folded into a codex dictated how writing—and later printing—would be positioned upon the page. A single sheet (or bifolio) is folded into two leaves, called folios; if it is folded again, the four resulting leaves are quartos; if another fold produces eight leaves, they are octavos. The assembly, or gathering, of sixteen leaves is called a signature, and a group of signatures, a register. All terms continue to be used in the construction of books today.

From the invention of the printing press until the early nineteenth century and the advent of the Industrial Revolution, books were made without covers. At first they were sold unbound so that they could be transported easily in carts. If the owner of the book wanted to have it covered, he went to an independent artisan who would tailor a binding from vellum, leather, or slim wooden boards to his personal specifications. The practice continued, giving rise to the profession of bookbinder.

Once printing presses had evolved to accommodate large sheets of paper, printers realized that a number of book pages could be printed on a single sheet, which could then be folded to the size desired.

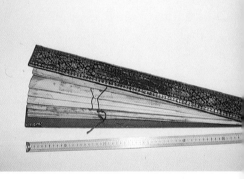

When folded in half, or in quarters, or into octavos or signatures of sixteen pages each, the paper could be secured with cord to hold the pages together. Stitches were based on three types of fastening: linking, lapping, or looping. Linked stitches ran across the backs of the signatures, attaching them directly to one another, but this type of stitch—a chain stitch—was vulnerable to unraveling. Lapped and looped stitches proved more durable because they doubled back on themselves, creating a common support for the signatures. Once the stitching was secure, the spine formed by the backs of the signatures was hammered and rounded so that, when the book was opened and the spine straightened, the pages would splay out evenly without undue pressure on the spine. The spine was reinforced with glue, and sometimes with tape (or, these days, with a special cotton mesh called crash), and the covers, or casing, were designed to fit around the assembly. Until fairly recently, signatures were left uncut; it was up to the purchaser of the book to slit the pages to ready the book for reading.

Casings vary, from primitive, decorated wooden battens (which are seen here on an old palm-leaf book) to hand-tooled leather casings like those below, which cover a set of books on our favorite subject – paper!

Bookbindings and the endpapers used to attach them to the body of the book could be exceedingly opulent. Usually crafted of leather, bookbindings were embossed and tooled with gold leaf in elaborate patterns. In the nineteenth century, publishers recognized the need to produce their own bindings; to gain acceptance with their audience, they stamped their mass-produced covers in gold and block-printed or marbleized endpapers in imitation of earlier techniques. In the Victorian era, the outside edges of the pages were often marbled as well.

Twentieth-century books come in all shapes and sizes, in hardbound and paperback editions. What about the twenty-first century? Some futurists predict that entire libraries will be housed in a single programmable book; using a reprintable digital ink, the paper will be able to be printed and erased over and over and over again, depending upon what you want to call up to read. We'll have to see it to believe it.

In the meantime, the traditionally bound, handmade book is enjoying a renaissance as an art form. The result can be conservative in appearance, to honor a like-minded piece of writing, or it can be wildly imaginative. One book might be folded in a simple accordion, while another might exhibit a flurry of different papers cut and shaped in myriad forms, then tethered with ribbon or raffia. Some artists' books contain no words at all but, instead, are adorned with collaged elements and hand-inked calligraphy. Although most artists' books are unique

In Italy, hand-blocked papers were tradition- ally used as endpapers; the Florentine firm of Giulio Giannini e Figlio also uses them to cover a variety of objects such as boxes, picture frames, and all manner of hand-bound personal books, including journals.

and idiosyncratic, some plain-page versions are results of collaborations with small presses who help produce and design them to be repositories of thoughts, reflections, and mementoes. Such diaries, journals, and scrapbooks testify to an artist's individual skills yet are produced to be accessible to many.

Our lives are like collages. Everything we do or say is not memorable, of course, but many telling moments can pass us by and become lost in the unpredictable haze of recollection unless we net them, like butterflies, and give them a place to rest. Fleeting moments caught on film can be preserved indefinitely on the acid-free leaves of a photo album or scrapbook. As storehouses for precious ephemera, including family photographs, ticket stubs, matchbook covers, and postcards, nothing can surpass these repositories of memory. A scrapbook may be as casually formatted as a three-ring binder or as carefully crafted as any fine, hand-tooled, leather-bound book. Some of the more elaborate memory books available today are bound with die-cut frames inside instead of pages; you simply insert pairs of photos

back-to-back into the frames. For posterity, it is best to choose an album with archival-quality, acid-free pages, separated by interleaves (thin sheets of waxed tissue that can be torn out once the adhesive securing the photographs or other mementos has dried). To preserve news clippings and other fragile items printed on acidic paper, photocopy them onto acid-free paper. Use archival adhesives, pH testing pens, and ecofriendly ink, too. And don't forget to label each photograph; future generations will want to know who everyone is in the picture. Simple headings can be spelled out with rubber-stamp alphabets. Items that will enhance a scrapbook include archival photo corners, pressed flowers or leaves, fragments of poems or other writings penned in colored or metallic inks, gold stars or stickers, and images pressed on the page with rubber stamps.

As our lives unfold, we find ourselves in a continuous dialogue with our inner selves. Most of us simply listen to our voices and get on with it, but others feel compelled for one reason or another to

Some contemporary library binders highlight their stitchery skills on the outside of their one-of-a-kind books (LEFT). When opened wide, a photograph album illustrates how its pages splay without injuring the spine.

"I BELIEVE IT IS A VERY USEFUL METHOD TO TAKE ACCOUNT OF EVERY DAY, HOWEVER UNPROFITABLE."

–**JOHN NEWTON**(1725-1807); **CLERGYMAN** AND AUTHOR OF "AMAZING GRACE"

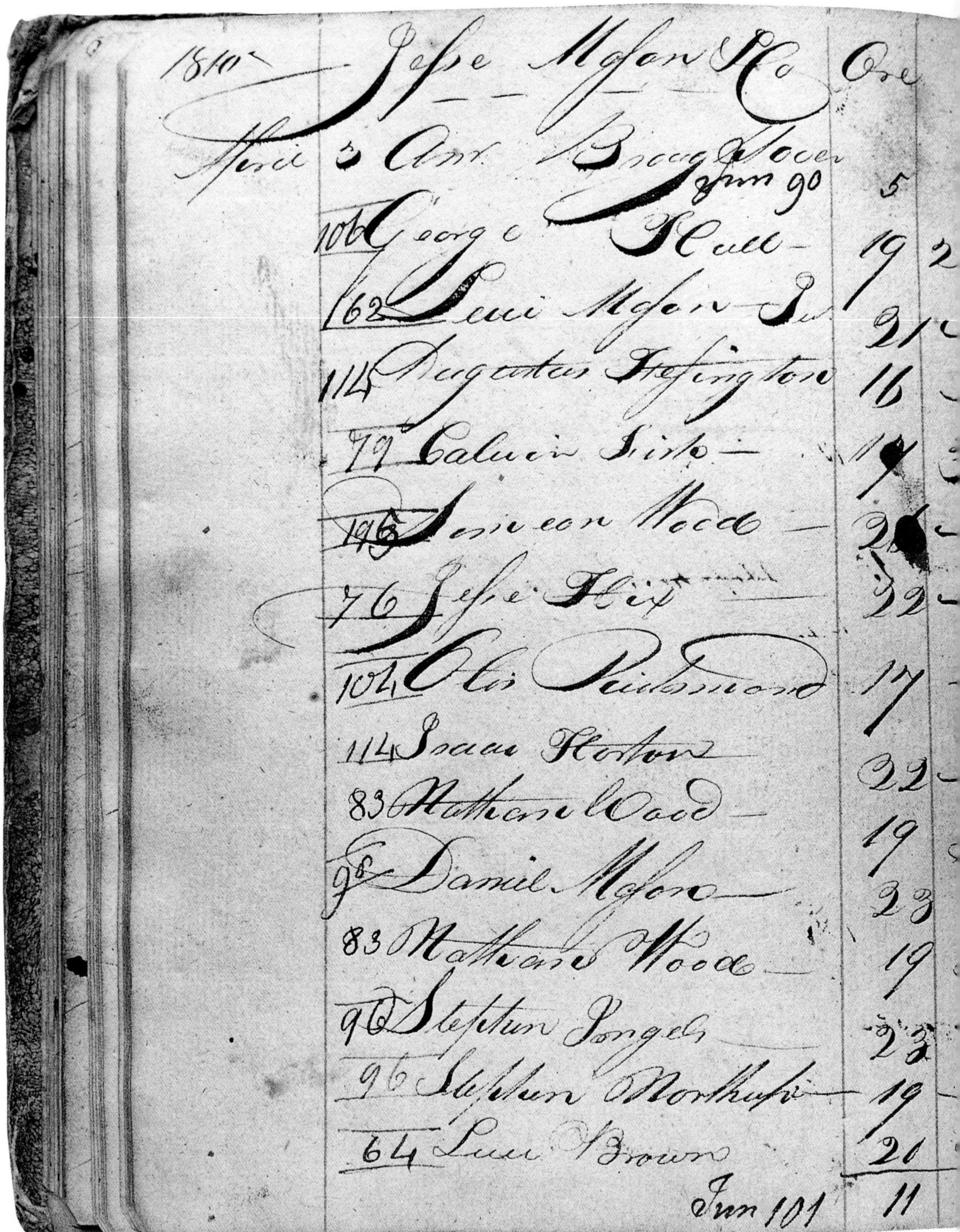

jot down their reflections. Although no one can pinpoint an exact date when the first diary might have
been written, journaling probably derived from the rendering of calendar-driven routines, such as the
keeping of household and/or commercial accounts and ships' logs.

In the hundred or so diaries he researched for his survey of the genre, *A Book of One's Own: People and Their Diaries*, Thomas Mallon separates diarists into seven categories: chroniclers, travelers, pilgrims, creators, apologists, confessors, and prisoners. In their 1997 exhibition *Private Histories: Four Centuries of Journal Keeping* the curators at the Pierpont Morgan Library in New York City organized the diaries on display according to the following themes: love (some of these were written in code or mirror writing to prevent or postpone disclosure), war, loss, hardship, youth, reflection, work, travel, portraits, and fiction. In fact, most diarists do not concentrate solely on one particular subject. Themes and preoccupations blur together.

Writing a diary can begin at any time and may continue for as long as it feels right. Many people feel the urge to start a diary as an outlet for an intensely emotional experience, such as falling in (or out of) love, while others might turn to a diary only to transcribe the events of a particular vacation, or to document the seasons in a garden. Still others use a journal to analyze their dreams. Whatever the reason, a diary is often treated with marked respect, with the choice of a beautiful blank book a decision that is well considered. Journals come in every size and shape, with or without ruled lines. Some are outfitted with locks and keys. In selecting a diary or journal, ask yourself: What feels good to my heart and hand? As a repository of your innermost thoughts, your journal should live up to—and beyond—your expectations.

The most quotidian of diaries are reserved for recording information that
might need to be referred to over and over again. Account books, in fact, are
the antecedents of the diaries we know today. Some other types of daybooks
or diaries you might write in include birthday/anniversary books, journals
documenting a baby's first year, and garden calenders. It is fun and informa-
tive to press botanicals between the pages of the latter. In fact, journaling is
like creating a collage–adding found objects contributes to the experience.

PAPER ENFOLDS
          OUR ASPIRATIONS AND DESIRES
WITHIN ITS GENTLE EMBRACE.

transformed by paper

          PAPER OFFERS OUR GRATITUDE,
TESTIFIES TO OUR RESPECT.
          PAPER EXHIBITS US AT OUR BEST
AND REVEALS OUR
          VULNERABILITY.

Paper is paradox. On the one hand it is simplicity incarnate. On the other, when paper is transformed into objects that appear sophisticated and complex in form, we can barely find words to describe its power. We ask ourselves: How can this two-dimensional material embody such limitless possibilities for creative expression? Perhaps we should simply regard paper, as Asian peoples do,

as sacred. Then the miracle of its ability to transform—and to be transformed—would be irrefutable. Paper has the innate ability to make us see differently, think differently, and act differently. Paper enhances a gift because paper is itself a gift—the ultimate gift.

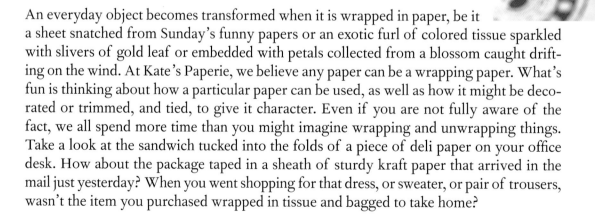

An everyday object becomes transformed when it is wrapped in paper, be it a sheet snatched from Sunday's funny papers or an exotic furl of colored tissue sparkled with slivers of gold leaf or embedded with petals collected from a blossom caught drifting on the wind. At Kate's Paperie, we believe any paper can be a wrapping paper. What's fun is thinking about how a particular paper can be used, as well as how it might be decorated or trimmed, and tied, to give it character. Even if you are not fully aware of the fact, we all spend more time than you might imagine wrapping and unwrapping things. Take a look at the sandwich tucked into the folds of a piece of deli paper on your office desk. How about the package taped in a sheath of sturdy kraft paper that arrived in the mail just yesterday? When you went shopping for that dress, or sweater, or pair of trousers, wasn't the item you purchased wrapped in tissue and bagged to take home?

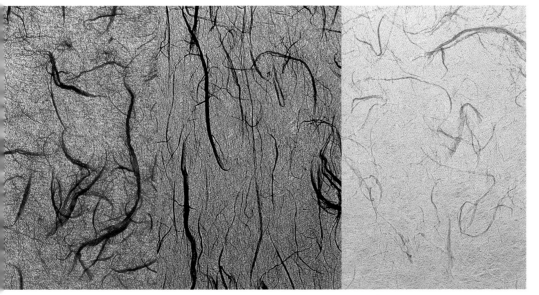

The transformation of paper can occur during the papermaking process – or afterward. In other words, the way paper looks can be changed at any time. Nepalese paper made from a type of Himalayan mulberry called **lokhta** has been block printed with hands bearing symbolic patterns; by contrast, translucent jewel-toned **unryu** papers exhibit fibers that were left intact within the paper as it was being made.

As long as paper has existed, in whatever form, some has been reserved or recycled for wrapping, particularly, at first, to protect perishable items such as foods and spices. For such utilitarian purposes, wrapping paper has typically been made of lesser-quality materials. The earliest instance of a wrapping paper on record dates from 1035 B.C., according to historian Dard Hunter, by a traveler to Egypt who was astonished by the array of packaged goods he found to be wrapped for transport, often with paper recovered from extra cloth that had been made to mummify the dead.

As has been noted in a preceding chapter, the basic steps in making paper are few. But the attitude toward paper and how it is made has differed markedly as the centuries have passed since its discovery in China. In the West, the appetite for paper has been guided by commercial imperatives. The urgency to increase production of currency, deeds, documents, broadsheets, newspapers, and books spurred the invention of the printing press and hastened the conversion from time-consuming handmade efforts to the rapid-fire manufacture of paper by machine. Quantity, not quality was—and in many cases still is—the criterion.

With today's renaissance of interest in fine paper and in the myriad ways paper can be used and enjoyed, people—and not just artists and designers—are working with paper in ways they might never

before have imagined. Before you embark on any project involving paper, you should learn the individual characteristics of the sheets of paper you hope to work with. Although paper is extremely accommodating and resilient, it also brooks few mistakes. You would not want an inkblot or tear to ruin a project to which you have dedicated a great deal of time and effort.

There are literally thousands of papers you can choose from. Kate's Paperie alone stocks thousands of handmade papers from all countries around the world. Here's a list of a few generic types of paper that are enjoyable to work with; some handmade and some manufactured by machine: tissue, tracing paper, watercolor paper,

parchment (or vellum), acetate, kraft paper, cover paper and card stock, origami paper, rice paper, and metallic paper, including foil.

The first rule of thumb is: buy more paper than you think you will need. Reserve a sheet or two for test runs and set aside a few extra sheets in case of inadvertent blunders. This advice applies equally to papers you are going to write on and to those you might consider folding, gluing, or decorating. Some papers are more porous than others. Some are sealed or saturated with a special moisture-resistant substance, called size, so that inks and paints will not bleed into or feather across the paper. Unsized papers are called by the term "waterleaf." As expected, they are very absorbent.

Strength and flexibility are not always indicated by the obvious thickness and/or transparency of a paper. Handmade papers exhibit a random grain called rough-shake. Because of this characteristic, a handmade paper tends to be stronger than its machine-made counterpart. Some tissue-thin, translucent handmade papers exhibit greater strength than their thicker, opaque coun-

terparts. A disadvantage of handmade papers is that they can wrinkle or come apart when they are glued or wet. Always test a sheet of handmade paper to see if it suits your project. Or cut a small sample off one corner if the sheet is larger than your project requires, and test the sample instead.

Machine-made papers follow a grain. The fibers run in one direction—the direction the slurry swims as it speeds along the machine bed. If you have ever tried to tear a clipping from a newspaper, you know that it is easier to rip the paper in one direction than the other. This is due to the grain. To test the grain of any machine-made sheet of paper, grip the sheet in both hands and bend it in both directions; you will meet greater resistance in the direction that goes against the grain. If you remain uncertain about the grain direction, tear a small square from a corner of the sheet in question. Mark one edge of the sample as well as the equivalent edge on the "parent" sheet. Dampen the sample; it will curl with the grain.

If you want to fold machine-made paper, try to do so with the grain. If you want to tear along the grain, make a sharp crease first. Heavy papers can be lightly scored to ease the fold. To do this, place a metal ruler along the line of the fold

But at Kate's Paperie, we feel that a box, if it is special, can also be a wrapper. These cylindrical mesh boxes from the Philippines are a case in point; they are so lovely that we snuggle gifts in tissue inside them, to let the recipient know that the boxes themselves are part of the gift.

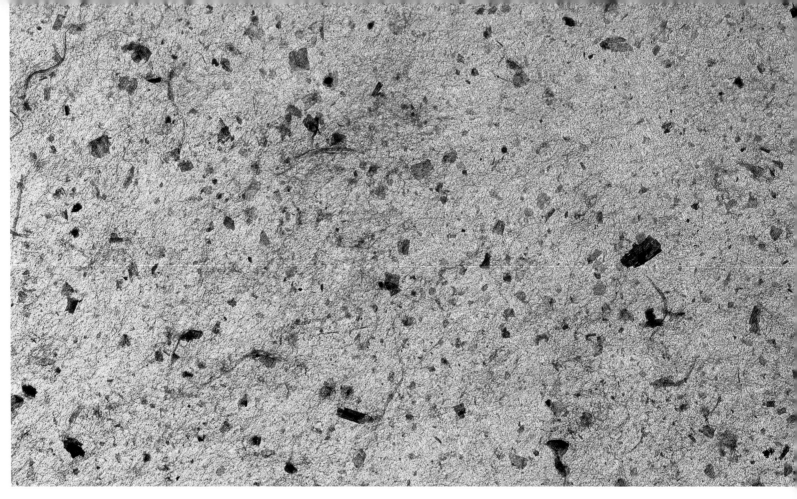

and lightly drag a pin or needle along the ruler to create a scratch. Bend the paper backward, away from the fold line; fold; and using the ruler, or a special tool made of plastic or bone called a bone folder, press down on the fold to flatten it. Before tearing the paper, fold it back and forth a few times to set the crease, then tear slowly and gently from the top of the crease to the bottom. Slightly dampening the fibers along the crease will result in a deckle edge.

Grain also affects gluing. Because glue (and paste) is moist, it will cause paper with a grain to expand or stretch along the grain. Glue can also cause paper to curl. For this reason, glue- and paste-moistened paper should be allowed to relax before affixing the paper to whatever it is meant to adhere to. This process should take a few minutes. You can literally see the paper let go of its surface tension.

When you buy a paper, you must, like the papermaker, consider how important several factors are to you, notably the finish (or surface quality), the absorbency, and the weight. There are, for instance, three types of finish: (1) *Rough* describes the natural state of the paper; rough papers may also be termed coarse, *antique, felt,* or *irregular.* (2) *Not,* referring to the longer phrase "not hot pressed," is a term that is interchangeable with a wide range of synonyms, including some familiar to anyone who has worked with house paints—*eggshell, matte,* and *satin.* Other terms you may encounter are *unglazed, velour, cold-pressed, medium, regular,* and *slightly grained.* (3) A *smooth hot pressed,* or *H.P.,* finish results from pressing the sheet between hot glazing rollers or cold, highly polished rollers. H.P. papers are also categorized as *glazed, high sheen,* or *supercalendered.*

Unless it is intentionally textured, a paper should be smooth and free of irregularities, the most common of which include lumps and knotted fibers. A defective paper may also exhibit indentations or ridges, especially along an edge, and it may be uneven in its thickness. (Intentional inconsistencies are called wildnesses or peppering, and include embedments, such as fibers or confetti.) None of the above defects, other than embedments, should be tolerated in a fine-quality paper.

To reduce the absorbency of paper and prepare it for inks, a starch or gelatinous, glue like substance, called size or sizing, may be added to the wet pulp when it is in the beater. Size also can be applied to the surface after the paper has dried. A paper needs to be properly sized for you to write upon it without fearing that the ink will blur across or into the sheet.

Paper is measured by weight, but weights can be deceptive; as they are calculated by the number of sheets—and, of course, sheets vary widely in size as well as in thickness or density. Bulky paper tends to be porous and, therefore, lighter in weight, even though it is thicker. Weight in and of itself will probably not affect your decision about what paper to buy, though thickness might.

The choice of one paper over another can alter your perception of what might be enclosed within. Surprising papers, such as silk tissue teamed with a Remondini paper from Italy in a nineteenth-century endpaper design – used to enfold a loaf of bread BELOW LEFT – shifts one's focus towards the bread from commonplace object to sublime gift. Handmade papers, such as a granular-looking Japanese **chiri** paper, OPPOSITE, or a paper embedded with pungent bits of chili pepper, BELOW RIGHT, are subtle accomplices to the art of giving.

Lastly, if you are planning to purchase sheet paper in quantity, it may already be prepackaged. A quire, for example, contains 24 sheets; a mill pack, either 100 or 125 sheets; and a ream, 480 (sometimes 500) sheets, or 20 quires. Bond paper and computer paper is usually sold in packages of 500 or 1,000 sheets.

Buying paper is a sensual experience. A sheet of paper should look right to your eye, but it should also feel right—and sound right, smell right, and, perhaps, feel good to the tongue! Hold your paper up to the light. If it is translucent, how do the fibers lie? Are they evenly distributed across the surface of the sheet? If the paper is reflective, does the surface sheen appear smooth and unmarred? Does the underside of the sheet differ from its topside, and is this intentional? Is the watermark, if any, distinct? Shake the sheet. Does it feel crisp and well balanced? Does it make a satis-factory sound as it is shaken? Does it fold, crease, and tear evenly? Is absorbency an issue? If so, test a small sample of the paper by moistening it. If you are uncertain about the paper you've chosen, buy extra sheets and experiment.

There are many things you can do to change how a piece of paper looks. If you make your own paper by hand, you can add all sorts of enhancements to the slurry, such as flower petals, leaves, seeds, confetti, and bits of string or ribbon. The only thing to remember with these is that they should be lightweight and relatively flat.

A ready-made paper can be altered in a number of ways, too. Among these are folding, crinkling, tearing, cutting, piercing, and embossing. And, of course, a sheet of paper can be made to look different when it is decorated, or when it is cut up and used as a decorative element, as in collage or paper weaving.

PAPER, LIKE SKIN, FAIRLY BEGS TO BE CARESSED. ITS TACTILE SURFACE SINGS UNDER YOUR FINGERTIPS.

It is best to fold with the grain of the paper, pulling the pressing instrument, such as a ruler or bone folder, from the top of the paper toward you. Folds can be made, like pleats in a kilt, to fall in the same direction, or they can alternate directions in the manner of box pleats. Pleats may vary in width; spaces between box-style pleats don't have to be uniform, either. Soft, unpressed folds are known as flutes. These give the surface of the paper a pretty scalloped appearance, one that might particularly suit a lamp shade. Because flutes will flare if they are not held in place, the fluted sheet must be glued to a second, supporting sheet of paper. Apply glue to the flat paper bands between the flutes; press to affix.

Thin papers, like the tissue shown on these pages and crepe paper, benefit from folding, and also from being crinkled. Once you crinkle a paper, it can be flattened with a warm, not hot,

iron. The textural effect created by a network of crinkles dramatically partners a crisp, smooth paper when the two papers are curled around a present that cannot be wrapped in a conventional manner, such as a bottle of wine. Crinkles can be given additional visual interest by tie-dyeing. As the dye saturates the paper it clings to the crinkles, which then come up darker than the surrounding area.

Rips and tears may turn out ragged or tidy, depending upon whether you are working with or against the grain. Tightly creasing a fold along the tear line will ensure a neater edge along your tear. After folding the paper, insert a metal

Tissue is one of the most compliant of papers; it can be folded or scrunched, and even shredded, to no adverse effect. Even when it is deeply saturated with color, tissue appears semi-transparent, so gathering or layering two or more sheets will give a wonderful three-dimensional effect.

Ancient marbled papers were considered works of art worthy of framing on a wall; indeed, a gift of marbled paper was considered a token of esteem. Enduring patterns include the pebbly-looking ones resembling stones and the feathery ones called peacock. Because marbling inks sit upon the surface of the sheet, these papers must be carefully creased before they are folded or they will scrunch, and sometimes break, along the fold.

ruler into the crease; tear the paper carefully from out to look quite filmy along the edge of the paper. More aggressive rips will liberate individual fibers for a feathery appearance.

Making incisions in paper adds the illusion of a third dimension, especially when the cuts, such as *X*s, arcs, or triangles, are folded back on themselves to create flaps. A sharp blade is essential to a clean cut. Use a utility or matte knife, or an X-Acto knife, and change the blades as frequently as necessary. Always back the paper with a resilient cutting mat as you work. A mat will hold the paper steady and it will protect the work surface from nicks. To avoid accidents, turn the paper just enough so that you are not cutting directly toward yourself, and make sure your fingers are out of range of the blade. To effect a neat cut, always premeasure and mark the positions of the cuts. Use a metal ruler to guide each incision. Thicker papers may require a second or third pass of the blade. Without moving the ruler, gently test the cut with the point of the blade. If you meet resistance, that means the knife has not fully penetrated the paper.

The traceries achieved by piercing a sheet of paper can be very graceful and are especially handsome when light shines through them; larger punched holes may be arranged in more dramatic patterns. All you need to create your own pattern is a sharp-pointed object that can comfortably perforate the paper. Narrow-gauge knitting needles and leather crafters' awls work well, as do nails. Because piercing is viewed inside-out—that is, with the bumpy part facing outward—patterns must be transferred onto the back of the paper. This, of course, means that any realistic pattern will be transmitted backward. Draft the outline of your design ahead of time on a sheet of tracing paper. Flip the tracing paper and place it facedown on the sheet of paper, which should itself be placed facedown on felt or another soft surface that has a bit of give.

As mentioned in the section on printing, embossing is a process whereby a die is pressed into a dampened sheet of paper to create a pattern with a raised surface. You can emboss a single figure or motif into the paper, or repeat it over and over to generate a textural effect. You can also press the entire sheet against or into a textured material to transmit its pattern to the paper.

Other decorative techniques involve coloring or dying the paper. Marbling and stamping are just two of these. The earliest form of marbling, called *suminagashi*, originated in Japan. Equated with piety

and used as a background for calligraphy, *suminagashi* is said to have been inspired by a courtly game whereby colored inks eased by brush into water were blown by mouth into a design that could be lifted off the water when it came into contact with an absorbent paper. In the mid-fifteenth century, Persian and Turkish practitioners of the art called the nebulous-looking swirls they created *abri* or cloud art.

In the marbling process, drops of paint are held in suspension on the surface of a liquid, typically water thickened with a food-additive size called carrageenan. (The size prevents the paint from sinking too far into the water.) A marbling comb or rake is passed back and forth across the floating drops, and then from side to side (and/or diagonally) to create the pattern desired. A sheet of paper sponged with alum—a mordant that allows the pigments to bond upon its surface—is laid gently upon the marbled pattern. When the paper is lifted off, the marbled pattern clings to the surface.

The Chinese stamped paper as early as the seventh century A.D., and the technique continues to be an exciting way to decorate the surface of a paper. The main thing to keep in mind is how you want the stamped image to look. Do you want to place a single stamped impression on the sheet, or repeat it over and over to create a pattern? A pattern can run around the border of the sheet, or it can be repeated over its entire surface. If you are going to create a pattern, do you want the images to abut, or do you want to leave space around them? Negative areas can make as much of an impact as the image itself.

You can make a stamp from almost any material that will hold paint or ink. Children enjoy creating stamps from potatoes or cellulose sponges; they often graduate to linoleum blocks when they become adept at cutting. Rubber stamps come in hundreds of patterns, or you can order one made to your specifications. If you are handy with a linoleum tool, you can make your own rubber stamp from an eraser. The only caution: Don't cut too much too fast.

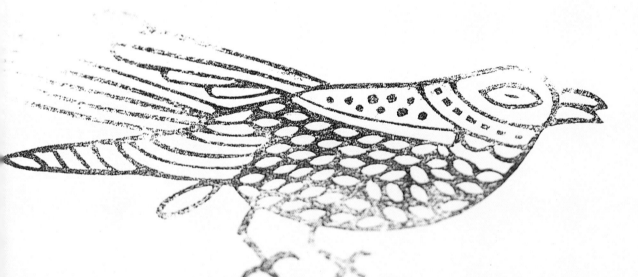

Working with a rubber stamp of her own design, Theresa Case, of New York City-based Stars and Eggplants, creates repeat patterns on recycled papers such as butcher paper and so-called bogus paper, which are typically used for packing. Her soy-based inks are so nontoxic they are favored by the food industry as color enhancers. As can be seen from the Nepalese wood-blocked birds LEFT AND BELOW, any imprint will appear in the reverse on paper.

Many people come into Kate's Paperie in search of the perfect paper to commemorate a special event. A wedding is the most obvious example of such an affair, but birthdays, holidays, and religious rites such as confirmation or, bar/bat mitzvah also inspire a yearning to create something unique to the occasion. Oftentimes that special something is an invitation or a card, but it can also be a beautiful work of art or something crafted and decorated in a special way. When something is intentionally made to be

"'DID SOMEONE REALLY CUT
THIS OUT BY HAND?'
        THE CHILDREN KEPT ASKING.
'REALLY?' THE EYEBROWS
        AND MUSTACHE,
            THE FIERCE WRINKLES
BETWEEN THE EYES,
THE FACE, ALL WERE THE
        MEREST BLACK WEBS.
            HIS OPEN HAND HAD BEEN
CUT OUT FINGER BY FINGER.
THROUGH THE SPACES
            YOU COULD SEE
        LIGHT AND THE ROOM
        AND EACH OTHER."

    – MAXINE HONG KINGSTON
        THE WOMAN WARRIOR

one of a kind, it celebrates both donor and recipient. Because we celebrate paper here at Kate's Paperie, honoring the ceremonial aspects of paper comes naturally to us. In doing so, we follow in a tradition as old as paper itself.

In China, colorful and elaborate paper cutouts representing myriad forms, such as fictional characters, animals, flowers, and even the Great Wall, are ritually given out at festival times to be pasted everywhere as good luck charms. OVERLEAF The Japanese kite known as **yakko**, the footman, features a diamond on each wing, which symbolizes family. Kites clear the air for an auspicious new year; indoors, they protect the house against fire – a marked concern in a nation where most dwellings are constructed of wood and subdivided with wood-and-paper screens.

Using paper in artful and decorative ways to appease gods or to impress authority figures is central to ceremonies practiced by many cultures that communicate via this medium. One might argue that this occurs because paper can be found almost anywhere and is affordable to all but the destitute. But it also occurs because, in some cultures, and especially those of the Far East, paper is considered to be sacred. On an elemental level, paper represents the quintessence of the magical merger of the ordinary and the sublime. Because paper may be made from bark, stalk, husk, leaf, and other vegetable substances, it is rooted to the earth. Paper is also thought to be divine because fire translates it into ash. As smoke curls heavenward, it carries messages and fervent wishes to the gods; spirits may themselves temporarily dwell in that smoke. Paper is the ideal medium for bringing the worldly and the spiritual aspects of ceremony into harmony.

If you travel around the world, you will encounter many festivals that are dramatized by and celebrated with ceremonial paper. December 6, for example, is the feast day dedicated to Saint Nicholas in a number of European countries. In one Swiss village, the miter the saint wore is reproduced as a giant paper hat, the front of which is pierced to accommodate a flickering candle worn behind. The glowing miters are worn in a parade to honor this holiday.

At the November festival known as Loy Krathong, the people of Thailand float little paper boats folded into the shape of lotus blossoms on the rivers to carry off their troubles; the lotus boats hold candles, which twinkle on the water. To the Japanese, the natural cycles of life, death, and rebirth are contained in paper. Spotless white paper embodies the conjoined notions of innocence and birth; shaped and folded, paper expresses the idea of presence or being; burnt, it transports spirits to the heavens and signals rebirth. Of all Japanese festivals, none is more elaborately celebrated than the New Year. A sacred taboo rope, woven of rice straw, that rebuffs evil spirits and encourages good fortune is strung across the entrance to every temple and home; the ropes

are hung with paper streamers called *gohei*, which are folded in zigzag designs. *Harai-gushi*, a cross between a pom-pom and a broom, is twitched back and forth in the air to sweep away demons and sanctify the space where a ceremony is to be conducted. Temple and family altars are decorated with paper cutouts.

The Japanese New Year is marked also by the delivery of greeting cards that convey good wishes, as well as by games. Paper kites are flown; giant versions may be burned to ensure prosperity and safety during the coming months. Competition is fierce to see who will excel at a literary game entailing the recall of a hundred traditional poems written on paired poem cards called *hyukuniisshu*. Cards displaying the endings of the poems are placed faceup in front of the players; as the opening lines of each poem are recited, the players vie to see who will be the first to complete the poem and pair it with its matching card.

Some believe that the kite, beloved as a form of play and as a pastime in many countries, may have originated in China, where it was thought to function as an emissary between earthbound humans and the gods residing in heaven. Others feel that kites might have their origins in the South Pacific, and perhaps in Malaysia and Indonesia, where kites were, and are, made of leaves. Kites figure prominently in cultures throughout the Far East, particularly in Japan, where the national enthusiasm for kites reached its apogee in the eighteenth century. In Japan, kite flying remained an exclusively male activity for centuries. By tradition, kites were offered to a couple on the occasion of the birth of their first son, and were later given to boys on their own special festival day. One shape that is emblematic of this particular festival is the gaily painted carp wind sock, which "swims" with the wind like the fish of legend that swam to heaven and became a dragon. Because it symbolizes courage and ambition, the carp is considered a particularly auspicious totem for sons.

Cutting paper for decorative purposes is an age-old craft, and one that is associated with many folk traditions in which cutouts were used to lend significance to religious or ceremonial occasions. In India, for example, cut-and-folded paper stars are hung in honor of the festival called Diwali. Germans practice the intricate cut-paper craft called *scherenschnitte* ("silhouettes") and the Poles create designs they call *gwiazdy*. In China, stacks of thin paper are pinned together and stamped as a single unit to create cutouts inspired by scenes from everyday life and other subjects. American doilies, popular as Valentine adornments, follow in the paper-cutting tradition, too.

OPPOSITE Mexicans celebrate the memory of their ancestors during the festival known as El dia de los Muertos – the Day of the Dead – with ghoulish images punched out on bright tissue-paper banners, called **papel picado** or **estampas**; with which they decorate home and altar. Here they embellish the windows of the Mexican restaurant "Mi Cocina" in New York.

In Japan, paper is not merely an object; it is a concept. Paper is not something to be taken for granted. Instead, it is held in great esteem. Paper is useful, of course, but because it willingly adapts to many other uses besides communicating a message, and because it can be recycled, paper represents the idea that ordinary things and everyday life can and should be revered. From the shoji panels that filter light into the Japanese home to the colorful, multi-ribbed parasols that deflect sun and

The presentation of gifts as a mark of love, honor, or respect is an age-old practice—everywhere in the world. In this painting by the Japanese artist Katsukawa Shundo, dating from around 1790, a man offers a women a small green box tied round with cord. If the gift looks familiar to us today it is because most of our wrapped and tied gifts are remarkably similar in their appearance.

rain shower alike, paper permeates virtually every facet of Japanese life. At Kate's Paperie, we honor this concept. Paper, to us, is something to be savored and exalted every single day.

Termed the "mirror of the soul," paper, in Japan, is considered to be a symbol of civilization, of culture, and of beauty. From the very moment paper was introduced into Japan in the seventh century, it has been held in awe and accorded a special reverence. The original character for paper, *kami*, is equivalent to the term for "up," signifying this sacred nature; white paper is identified with the purity of the shrine. Earliest paper, made from hemp and reserved for the the aristocracy and priests, was made to disseminate Buddhist sayings as well as imperial decrees. Paper was used also for the manufacture of light armor for samurai warriors. Over time, papermaking was removed from the influence of Buddhist monks and papermaking centers were established to create a wide variety of papers for all kinds of writings as well as for products such as parasols, fans, lanterns, kites, and dolls. All these items continue to be manufactured today.

By tradition, papermaking in Japan has always been guided by the cycles of nature and the seasons. The finest-quality handmade papers, called *washi*, are still made during the winter, when river water runs cold and snow covers the mountainsides and riverbanks. The papermakers trained in making *washi* repeat the steps and replicate the rituals that have been handed down for generations.

The *washi* papers known as *Echizen* have been made for fifteen hundred years in the village of Goka in the province of Kurodani in northern Japan. With its waterfalls and ample supply of the mulberry shrub known as *kozo*, Goka is ideally situated for papermaking. (Other perennial shrubs used for handmade papers include *mitsumata* and the rare *gampi*, but *kozo* is particularly appreciated for the length and strength of its fibers.) When ready for harvest, *kozo* stalks measure twenty-four to thirty-six inches long, and one inch in diameter. Once harvested, the stalks are bundled together and soaked or steamed to loosen the dark outer layer of the bark so that it can be peeled from the white woody inner layer. The inner layer, called *shirokawa*, is first dried in the sun and cleaned, and then roughly beaten to loosen the fibers. The fibers are then simmered and agitated in an alkaline solution in a ratio of ten to one (water to pulp) for two to four hours. (The choice of alkali depends on the type of paper desired; one that is often used is soda ash.) At Goka, the cooking of the pulp is a ceremonial ritual that takes place in a nearby shrine on the Lunar New Year. Traditionally, the cooked, softened, rinsed pulp was spread out on a snowbank, both to bleach it naturally in the sun and to keep it moist and cool until the papermaker was ready to work with it. Today, most paper mills rely on faster-acting chlorine. When it is ready to be used, the pulp is rerinsed and strained, and then beaten once again with a long mallet or club on a wood or stone surface to separate and roughen up the fibers. During this process, the papermaker constantly fingers the fibers, testing their resiliency to make sure none are cut or broken; the aim is to achieve a blend of fibers that will disperse evenly in water.

The beaten pulp is transferred to the wood papermaking vat, which is filled with cold water. The ratio of water to pulp varies depending upon the thickness of the paper to be made from that particular

The Japanese folded-paper forms called **noshi** stand in for rare objects; **noshi** are traditionally fastened with **mizuhiki**, which are stiff, tightly twisted paper strings dyed in special, ceremonial color combinations, such as red-and-white or gold-and-silver. All folds, ties, and knots are guided by rules of etiquette. It is imperative, for instance, that folds run in the correct direction—i.e., to the right—or they will signify death. ABOVE LEFT For informal wraps, silk-screened decorative papers such as these bellybanded **yezen-shi** and **wazome** rice papers are widely used.

batch of pulp. A ratio of 99 percent water to 1 percent fiber is not uncommon. The papermaker swirls the mixture by hand to disperse the fibers. At this point a bonding agent called *neri*, a viscous, starchy mucilage extracted from the roots of an okralike species of hibiscus or from the strawberry geranium plant, is added to the mixture. The *neri* slows the seepage of water through the screen in the papermaking mold, thus allowing the papermaker more time to make sure the fibers are rough-shaken evenly over the screen.

BASIC
ORIGAMI
FOLDS

UNFOLD   APPLY PRESSURE   EQUAL DISTANCES   FOLD DOT TO DOT   TURN OVER

The *neri* also prevents the fibers from tangling. The papermaker determines the amount of neri he needs by instinct or feel. Because many *washi* papers will renew their absorbency once they've dried, a small amount of kaolin, or clay, may be added to the pulp if a less porous surface is desired.

The mold for making the paper is essentially a hinged, handled wooden frame fitted with a flexible, removable screen woven of bamboo or reed splints shaven toothpick thin and held together by silk threads. An overhead suspension system functions as a counterbalance to the mold, which can be heavy. With a flick of his wrists, the papermaker rocks the frame back and forth in the vat, adroitly skimming off with each dip the exact amount of pulp required for a single layer. Layers of pulp become laminated to one another on the screen until they build up to a desired thickness. Because the *neri* renders the sheet resistant to water, and therefore to sticking, the sheets of paper may be stacked directly one upon another as they are lifted off the mold. Even so, a thread is often inserted between sheets to assist in lifting them off the stack after pressing.

The stack is left to stand overnight so that the *neri*, along with some of the water, may begin to seep out. The next day, the stack is gently pressed until 30 percent of the moisture is removed. The papermaker then brushes each sheet onto a board fashioned from gingko wood, using a wide horsehair brush called a *hake*. Corners of the sheet may be lightly glued to the wood to prevent it from slipping. If the papermaker is following traditional practice, he or she will take the boards outdoors and tip them toward the sun so that the paper can dry naturally. Sunlight strengthens the sheets and bleaches them still further. Drying takes about an hour, but some papermakers follow the faster, more modern practice of drying paper on a steam-heated metal surface. Once dry, the sheets are peeled off the board and stacked for shipment. At this point, a sheet of *washi* is ready for use.

CREASE AND UNFOLD   MOUNTAIN   FOLD UNDER   VALLEY   EQUAL ANGLES   EXISTING CREASE

To the Japanese, the essence—or presence—of paper is revealed in the act of folding it. This simple gesture transforms paper from a two-dimensional object into a three-dimensional one. Coincidentally, folding also makes a paper stronger. Folding paper around an object, such as a pair of chopsticks, or around foodstuffs, herbs, and medicines guarantees cleanness. By the same token, the ritual use of cut and folded strips of paper is a testament to the presence of a deity. Folded papers and paper cutouts are used as talismans, amulets, and charms to ensure good health and luck and to exorcise demons. As cult objects, folded strips, called *gohei*, adorn temples and shrines as well as the aprons of sumo wrestlers.

By the year 1000, the Japanese had developed the twin arts of folding paper known as *origata* and *origami*. Even when interpreted to purely utilitarian ends, a folded wrapping, called *origata*, is still considered an art form. When wrapping a gift, the *origata* is as essential to the gift as what is contained therein. How the gift is to be presented depends upon three factors: the gift, its recipient, and the occasion.

The gift package, inside and out, is treated with reverence and respect. Paper folding follows a strict etiquette, especially for objects created for a ceremonial purpose such as a wedding. By tradition, the act of creating a beautiful wrapping represents a visual expression of civility and good breeding. It also confirms that the gift within the wrapping is heartfelt. The wrapping itself expresses the character of the paper selected by the donor. Factors such as its color, its flexibility, its texture, and how the paper is

When creating an origami shape, such as the traditional crane (which is itself the symbol of origami),
the actual act of folding and the step-by-step sequence of making the folds assume just as much
importance as the object itself – if not more – because the folding adds not only another dimension to
the paper, but also another dimension of meaning through its powers of association. The folding of one
thousand cranes, for example, signifies good luck. Origami brooks no waste; although most origami are
folded from single sheets of paper, some complex shapes require two or more sheets.

cut, as well as the way it can be folded, all come into play. The folds may result in a *tato*, or decorative envelope, or a bag or a box. An ancillary folded object, such as a fan, or a symbolic object rendered in origami may be added to accent the package.

Printing on the paper, if any, is integrated into the design, as are embellishments such as closures and flaps. Some papers simulate other materials or textures, such as stone; such trompe l'oeil effects add to the intrigue and ceremony surrounding the presentation of the gift. Cords and ties, called *mizuhiki*, which were originally conceived as protective devices to inhibit impurities from tainting the contents of a package, may be enhanced by plaiting or by knots that exhibit special meanings. Paper may also be sliced into bands to fit snugly, like ribbon, around the package.

The opening of a package is honored, too, as a ritual act. Many packages enjoy the interplay of what is revealed and what is concealed, with hinges, flaps, or cuts hinting at the contents without disclosing them altogether until the very last minute.

The Japanese take an ecological as well as an artistic approach to their wrapping, so most packages are designed to be reused. A work of art, after all, should be enjoyed for a long time.

The folded articles known as origami are often used to decorate or accent a gift. They are also a pastime and endless source of amusement. Many classic shapes such as the crane, the frog, and the crab are invested with symbolism and engender powerful associations in the eye of the beholder. Some of these associations may be of a sacred nature, such as the concepts of longevity and peace inspired by the crane, while other connotations may simply emerge from the shape itself, such as the idea of balance and flight contained within the silhouette of a bird or a dragonfly. Other origami are frankly fun and have no religious or ceremonial significance at all.

Although origami shapes number in the thousands, all are predicated on a pair of elementary folds, the peak and the valley; a few basic folds utilizing these, such as the pocket, the hood, and the stair step; and several slightly more complex shapes that translate into a multitude of forms. Folds can also be pinched, pulled, twisted, and curled to artistic effect.

The Tokyo-based ribbon
manufacturer Mokuba pro-
duces two thousand new
ribbon designs each year.
Technological advances have
encouraged the company
to create such artful effects
as ruffling and pleating in
the same gossamer-fine
iridescent organza, which
gives the ribbon an extra
glimmer and gleam, depending upon how it is tied.

We all know the feeling of wonder and delight that's stirred up when we are presented a gift that is beautifully wrapped in a delicious paper and tied up prettily in a silken ribbon or shimmery cord. Like dance, the feeling awakened in us is as physical as it is emotional. There's the tension of anticipation, the surge of excitement as ribbons are untied and wrappings peeled back, and finally the gasp of discovery and sigh of pleasure released upon encountering the treasure, large or small, that has been secreted inside.

"GIVING PRESENTS IS A TALENT; TO KNOW WHAT A PERSON WANTS, TO KNOW WHEN AND HOW TO GET IT, TO GIVE IT LOVINGLY AND WELL."

To the Japanese, the idea of wrapping a package parallels the concept of enclosure, or "gentle concealment," that is represented by many aspects of their everyday and spiritual life and culture—from the shoji screens that contain but never confine an architectural space to rice scooped into and covered by a lacquerware bowl and lid. The screens respect the space; the bowl and lid dignify the food. What is enclosed, the manner in which it is enclosed, and the manner in which it is slowly and subtly revealed all bear equal weight. To conceal and then gradually unveil an object, or a room, or an aspect of nature, such as a garden or a view, is to testify to its innate beauty. It also testifies to the reverence with which the ritual of achieving the gentle concealment is held, as well as to the esteem held for the ultimate beholder of that object or room—or gift.

The Japanese confer upon the concept of wrapping the term *tsutsumi*—a word that derives from the principle of discretion and restraint that guides the way in which they ideally attempt to interact with one another. It is said that the first wrapped gift in Japan, tied round with a red rope secured with a red seal, was presented to the emperor of Japan by the ambassador from China in the eighth century. The wrap, tie, and seal testified to the spiritual purity of the contents contained therein. The notion of purity was perpetuated thereafter by the use of unadulterated white *washi* paper and by *mizuhiki* cords made from tightly twisted and starched strands of paper. White is the color of the gods; a crease in *washi* paper will retain its shape indefinitely; a *mizuhiki* knot cannot be untied without visible effort. A meticulously wrapped and tied package, therefore, symbolized the great effort that was taken to make sure the object within was free of impurities and, thus, truly represented the esteem with which the donor held the recipient of the gift.

Over time, the concept of *tsutsumi* grew ever more complex in scope. The strict etiquette governing the ritual of gift giving and the art of gift wrapping, or *origata*, required that each and every category of object be subjected to its own specific guidelines and rules. Each individual occasion, too, had its own style of wrapping, depending upon who was being celebrated, for what, and when. Today, although many rules have been relaxed, the respect for *tsutsumi* and *origata* still serves to motivate the presention of all categories of objects, and especially gifts.

Mokuba numbers over four hundred thousand snippets of ribbon in its archives, including those collected in some 650 sample books from France dating from 1836 through 1969. All are housed in Mokuba's private collection in Tokyo. The archives inspire many variations on traditional designs, such as the striped and the dotted ribbons shown FAR LEFT, OPPOSITE. Brand-new designs also enter the collection each year. The pure silk ribbon tied around the package THIRD FROM LEFT is by French couturier Jean-Paul Gaultier, who is renowned for his avant-garde color combinations. The Gaultier ribbon is so wide that many of Kate's Paperie customers intentionally purchase a yard or so to use as a scarf. OPPOSITE, NEAR LEFT Mixing two or three ribbons to create a soft multilooped (or cross-looped) bow is one way to highlight a gift for a special occasion. Just make sure colors coordinate. OVERLEAF Two pinned ribbons are velvet corduroy.

Ryban, reban, riban, ruban. Ribane, rebane, rebayne. Reabande, rib-awnde, rebaund, rebende. Ribband. Whatever name it has gone by, ribbon has served as an elegant accessory for centuries, both in the Orient and in Western cultures. In medieval Europe, *ribaninges* served as badges or marks of distinction; bordering garments or worked into cockades and braided into horses reins, ribbons were marvelous adornments for a knight and his horse. Ribbons were a logical outgrowth of the silk industry and coincidentally were produced in the centers of the European silk trade, notably Lyons and Saint-Etienne in France, as well as in Basel, Switzerland, and Coventry, England. With the technological advances fostered by the Industrial Revolution, a ribbon loom became capable of producing up to forty ribbons simultaneously, some boasting elaborate surface decoration. Ribbon design diversified be-

yond straight trimmings to include braids, cord, and other passementerie. Today ribbon is made from a variety of fabrics woven from natural as well as synthetic fibers. Textures and the so-called hand modu-

late according to the fabric. Silk and faux suede may be as soft as a baby's skin; satin as glossy as the surface of a pool. Polyester is known for its shine and cotton/viscose suits the gently corrugated grosgrain that originated as a milliner's trim. Some of the most elaborate organza ribbons are both pleated and frilled; others are cross-dyed so that they appear iridescent. Some especially wide velvets are as plushy as fur. Edge treatments vary too, from simple cut edges to woven selvedges to tightly sewn borders dotted with picots; edges also may be wired so that the

Other forms of ties include cord, string, and twine. Traditionally, ribbons that were braided together to form a garland signified immortality; because such plaiting also connoted fulfillment, you might consider braiding colored or metallic cord to weave around a package, to convey the same enduring sentiments to someone you care about. Accent your braid with roses, which are symbols of affection. You can buy ready-made roses, such as the organdy one here, or make your own by coiling a stiff ribbon around and around itself.

HOW TO TIE A BOW

ribbon will hold its shape when it is tied into a bow or other forms. Ribbon can be purchased in many widths, from ¼-inch up to four inches; by definition, a ribbon that exceeds nine inches is called a sash. When used to girdle the waist of a little girl's dress, it is just that.

Ribbons, like all luxury goods manufactured in Europe, initially were made for the aristocracy. Like most luxury items, too, including lace and tulips, ribbons endured periods when they were fetishized and periods when they were banned. But they never went completely out of style. In the 1950s, Shoichi Watanabe, son of an illustrious Japanese weaver of silk obis, visited Paris and became enamored of the wealth of silk ribbons he found there. He discovered a trove of sample books dating from the seventeenth century, when ribbons were at the height of fashion in France. Purchasing these books, Watanabe decided to wed the art and craft of French ribbon design to Japanese technology. He opened his first manufactory in 1954; twenty-three years later he founded Mokuba, a Tokyo-based company that now produces over tens of thousands of ribbons, braids, narrow laces, and trimmings for a world market in the fields of couture, millinery, home decorating, theater de-

sign, and crafts, among others. Watanabe's daughter Keiko, responsible for the design, choice of color, weave, and material of the ribbons, oversees the introduction of two thousand new items each year. Some are inspired by the vast collection of historical ribbons amassed by her father; others evolve in response to trends in art, culture, and fashion.

Charming adornments can be fabricated from ribbon, including miniature fans and, of course, bows that are fancier than the standard single-loop ones we were all taught as youngsters. The easiest way to manipulate ribbon is by basting it with thread first along one edge. You can then draw the thread tight to gather the edge of the ribbon. This strategy works well for ruching a plain ribbon or for creating a miniature fan from a pleated ribbon. Once you have pulled the thread as tight as you like, knot it off so that it will not slip.

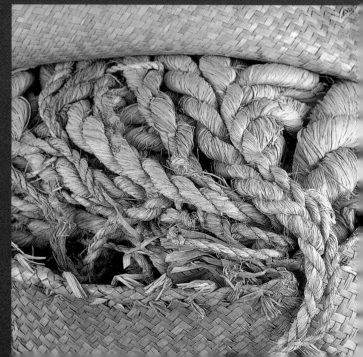

One of the easiest ways to tie a bow is to use two separate ribbons (STEP BY STEP, OPPOSITE) the two are crossed over each other at right angles, then tied together to form the bow. At Kate's Paperie, we follow the ancient Asian custom of tying lots of our packages with raffia. In Madagascar, where our raffia comes from, it is used ubiquitously, to tie everything. The raffia arrives in enormous bales measuring two and a half feet square by four and a half feet tall; each bale weighs 220 pounds! Inside are hundreds of hanks, which we must unwind to disengage individual strands. Raffia ties look best when you use several strands, as in the packages ABOVE, which sit in a nest of the same material.

Kate's Paperie is often approached by people who simply appear on our doorstep holding something they want to have wrapped in a special way. One man pulled a string of pearls from his pocket and asked how we could box and wrap it to make it as wonderful and unique as the person he wished to give it to; another wanted to create a present for his wife using one of our leather-bound journals as the "wrapping" for some cherished mementos of a trip they had enjoyed together. To many cultures, the wrapping and presentation of a gift is as much of a ritual as its purchase. Like an unfolding story, it is an experience to be delighted in, every step of the way.

We carry many varieties of boxes at Kate's Paperie. These are laminated with a **shalk** paper from Japan, which displays a subtle, variegated rib pattern. The triangular cutouts ease the lifting off the lids.

If we have learned anything from studying the cultural heritage of Japan, it is that the reverence with which the Japanese honor even the most humble objects—from a piece of gingerroot to an egg to a piece of paper—resonates deeply in both heart and soul. No matter how trifling or insignificant it may appear, an object is worthy of respect. No matter how simple or how small it may be, everything has value. Beauty is everywhere.

Contriving simple, utilitarian ways to protect and carry objects in order to enhance and preserve their integrity comes naturally to these practical people, who perceive innovation and recycling as inextricably fused. When Japan was still essentially a rural culture, people looked to the natural materials around them, such as rice straw, bamboo, various woods, rush, and hemp, to create packages for the things they had to transport from place to place. In doing so, they discovered that almost anything can be wrapped. Their system of packaging is still rooted in this agrarian and spiritual tradition.

Because the Japanese believe nature and the spirit to be united, the manner in which they wrap and tie an object carries an intrinsic symbolic message. They equate wrapping a gift with "wrapping the heart," so every gift is marked by thoughtfulness and consideration, both for the object housed within the container or wrapping and for the recipient of the gift. Bringing seemingly stark contrasts into harmony—like yin and yang—is central to the idea of any presentation. Rusticity and refinement, the transient and the eternal, the earthy and the sublime: such disparities are made evident—and rendered compatible—in choices of combinations of papers and ties that both emphasize and luxuriate in differences in texture as well as, perhaps, differences in color or pattern. A crinkled paper lashed with knotted cord, for example, reflects that approach, as would multiple layers of tissue interleaved with opalescent acetate bound with raffia.

The art of Japanese packaging extends to even the humblest objects, such as eggs. We adapted the concept of "how to wrap five eggs" to some wonderfully smooth ovoid erasers we picked up in Spain. We wrapped the erasers, in threes, in a crinkly mulberry paper called **moriki,** then secured the packages with twisted paper string that looks like a cross between raffia and **mizuhiki.**

The adage "It's the thought that counts," which was coined by the Hallmark Company of Kansas City, speaks to a Western take on the Eastern philosophy pertaining to giving from the heart. How a gift is wrapped does, indeed, reveal how much thought as well as effort went into selecting something special for a special someone.

Most gifts are presented in wrapped boxes. Although a box obviously protects the gift from damage while in transit, it can in and of itself be a beautiful object, and one worthy of saving and reusing. A few basic rules apply to boxing a gift. First and foremost, the box should securely enclose the gift; so its overall dimensions should match those of the gift as

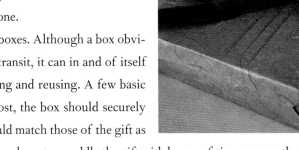

closely as possible. If the box is shaped, you may have to swaddle the gift with layers of tissue or another fine, flexible paper. The wrapping or box also should be sturdy enough to bear the weight of the object. Almost any paper that is pliant and resists tearing can be used to wrap gifts. Thick papers require a strong adhesive or tape to secure the folds in the paper so they do not break free. The Japanese tend to prefer wrapping paper around a box on the diagonal, so that the folds align along the edges of the box,

When wrapping a pleat-top package, make sure you cut enough paper to accommodate your pleats! Place the box faceup on the sheet and bring the two wide sides up around to the top of the package, leaving enough room on one side to make the pleats. Pleat that side, then lay the pleated side on top of the other side. Flip the package to hold pleats in place as you fold and tape ends shut. Turn the package faceup again and tie with a pretty ribbon, such as this organdy one from Mokuba.

with the final fold-over lying, like the flap of an envelope, across the front of the package. When folding in the conventional manner, they will often introduce one or more pleats into the design. The pleats function like slender pockets, into which a card or a folded origami such as a crane may be tucked. At Kate's Paperie, we custom-wrap boxed gifts with three pleats. To the Japanese, odd numbers connote celebration, while even numbers are associated with mourning. Celebration is also symbolized by having

the pleats face to the left (and mourning, by pleats to the right). Because gifts obviously are celebratory objects, the three pleats on our packages always face left. To indicate this, we tie a bow across the pleats so that its swallow-cut tails hang towards the bottom of the package.

Paper also can be folded and shaped, intentionally, in diverse ways to enhance the object that is to be wrapped. This is especially useful when you need or want to wrap something that is not going to be tucked into a box. Other containers that may be used to enclose a gift are baskets and pots, but you can also support a gift on something flat like a plate or a tray. Once you have established which paper or papers you want to use, consider how you may exploit the paper itself to the service of the overall design of your package. One technique is to layer one or more papers. Layered paper may be of a similar consistency, such as tissue, or you can combine two or more thicknesses and textures to capitalize on their discrepancies. Paper can be embellished or cut in various ways, too. You may want to integrate a stamped motif or text into your design, or you may want to add a slit to hold a gift card or tag. How do you want to close or seal the wrapping? How do you want to tie it up?

The forerunner of gift wrap, or "gift dressing," as we know it in the West was wallpaper, which had been made in England as early as 1509. But wallpaper, printed on thick paper, proved vulnerable to splitting and tearing, so packages were often covered in thinner paper or tissue. The Hallmark Company lays claims to what they call the accidental inception of gift wrap in the United States. In the 1920s, Joyce C. Hall set out some fancy French-made envelope linings in his Kansas City store to see if they would sell. Customers loved them so much, he decided to package them, three to a pack, as gift wrapping paper, for twenty-five cents. Today, commercial gift wrap can still be purchased in sheets; it can also be bought in rolls.

Unusual papers are wonderful allies when you want to wrap or set off an oddly shaped object. Natural-hued **sinamay,** a Philippine mesh woven from **abaca** (a banana plant), is coarse so it holds any shape, such as a rose (PREVIOUS SPREAD), nicely; it can also be scrunched to fit a container such as an oval wooden box, LEFT. Here, the **sinamay** gives the exotic fruits–an Israeli melon, a persimmon, and guava–an opportunity to breathe so that they will not rot prematurely. An especially crinkly paper from the Philippines perfectly matches up with an object, such as the chunks of bittersweet chocolate TOP, that might have a rugged profile; our collection of these papers comprises over a dozen colors. OPPOSITE Bags, of course, are the most adaptable of carrying cases for transporting a gift. Boxes may be tucked in them, or objects can be shrouded in a tissue or other pliable paper, like this ungeishi paper, and popped into the bag. Florists usually wrap up their bouquets in cones of paper; why not layer your own exotic paper over the florist's? Papers that coordinate with colors of the blooms are especially pretty.

As has been mentioned, specific paper objects are equated with ceremony in certain cultures. The Japanese folding fan called *sensu* is revered; its ribbed pleats allude to mountains and valleys, natural formations the Japanese hold sacred. When unfolded, the fan symbolizes prosperity. Thus it often accompanies a wedding gift to communicate a message of hope and good luck for the future bride and groom. Another object associated with the Japanese is the paper parasol. The parasol functions on a number of levels: it protects the head from sun; dyed red, which is the color associated with ceremony, and supported by the ceremonial quota of ribs—one hundred—the parasol is opened and raised during the tea ceremony; symbolizing dignity, the opened parasol is believed to temporarily house the deity. Both the fan and the miniature parasol are wonderful adornments for a gift.

Weddings inspire extra attention to detail when it comes to the wrapping and presentation of gifts and party favors. A diminutive gilt-edged envelope (the one above has been blown up twice its size) holding an even tinier gilt-edged enclosure can slide under a ribbon tied up into a frothy bow or be tucked into a pleat on top of the gift.

At the table, Jordan almonds, a symbolic treat associated with weddings, look especially inviting when rolled into cornucopias of translucent vellum. Traditionally, maidens would place a few of these sweets under their pillows so they would dream of their future beloveds.

In Europe during World War II, when cotton and wool were requisitioned for the military, some forms of clothing and a number of home-furnishing products were created from alternative materials. In Finland, for example, carpets were woven from straw and a twine fabricated from paper. Following in this tradition, textile artist Ritva Puotila creates floor mats woven with a weft of tightly rolled paper twine and cotton warp for the firm of Simplii Skandii.

In the abstract, a home is really
a collection of boxes, each of which
is decorated to express its owner's
personal taste and style. Paper figures
strongly in home decoration. In the
West we are familiar with such items as
wallpaper, folding screens, lamp
shades, tablecloths, and paper napkins.
In Japan, walls, windows, partitions
and lamps are made of paper and in
Korea, floors are covered with paper.
When adorned with paper, a room
is like a wrapped gift—a gift of the
spirit and a gift for the soul; a gift
for living.

When they were first invented in Europe, decorative papers were indistinguishable in terms of their eventual function. A hand-blocked or printed paper might be used, without particular discrimination, to decorate a wall,

to accent a ceiling, as an endpaper in a book, or to line a box. The earliest decorative papers were printed to simulate other materials. Paper used on the ceiling, for example, might resemble molded plaster, while paper decoupaged onto furniture would assume the appearance of marquetry or wood grain. Because it was printed by hand, paper was expensive—though not so costly as most of the materials it resembled. As a tool of mimickry, wallpaper initially was used in rooms of less importance. The aristocracy, of course, had no need to choose a less desirable material; they could afford the best. Only when wallpaper began to be perceived as ingenious and beautiful did it attain respect.

With the rise of a middle class and the building of more and finer dwellings that were owned rather than rented, the demand for home decoration grew, and the parallel trades of upholstering and paperhanging came into being. Once a machine was invented that could produce paper quickly and inexpensively by the roll rather than the sheet, wallpapers burgeoned in popularity. Initially, machine-made wallpapers continued to be printed in black and white and were colored in one of three ways: by overprinting

In the Victorian era, the British designer William Morris (1834-96) impacted the wallpaper industry to such an extent that no surface of a proper Victorian home remained untouched. The wall was divided into three distinct zones—dado, filling, and frieze—each separately papered; ceilings, too, were papered. Morris, a man of Renaissance accomplishments—he was also a notable poet, artist, printer, and craftsman—was also a social reformer who reacted to the ugliness spawned by the Industrial Revolution by promoting handcrafts. Many Morris designs for wall coverings continue to be produced today.

them with colors, by painting them in with a brush, or by filling them in with stencils. Over the centuries, wallpapers went in and out of favor according to fads and fancies in decor. The century spanning 1770 to 1870 marked the climax in appreciation for wallpapers, particularly for the exquisite hand-printed papers manufactured in France, where paperhangers were expert at hand-blocking and silk-screening. Wallpaper was one obvious decorative device by which the importance of a particular room could be demonstrated. Paper displaying a grandly scaled motif in a large repeat, therefore, was placed in the *salon*, while paper exhibiting more diminutive, allover patterns was used to decorate intimate spaces such as the *boudoir*, or bedroom.

Many motifs for decorative paper were inspired by textile designs, especially florals. While flowers painted in a naturalistic fashion appeared as fresh as if they had been snipped from the cutting garden, they also could be rendered in a stylized way as if woven into damask. *Trompe l'oeil*—fool-the-eye—papers imitating architectural elements or elaborate draperies, including laces, made their appearance during this period as well. Wallpaper often blended into an architectural scheme and served to highlight architectural elements of a room, such as a chimneypiece or the space over the door.

Once the province of stationers, wallpapers began, in the late eighteenth century, to be distributed and sold through paper hangers, and, in the early twentieth century, through a new breed of professional, the interior decorator. The fragile wallpapers of yesteryear have been replaced with washable, strippable, often vinyl-sealed wall coverings that are prepasted and pretrimmed so that they can be installed with ease. Coordinated fabric/wall-covering/wallpaper-border collections eliminate the hassle from the decision-making process.

Light is life. It bathes us and it warms us. Light guides and inspires; so does paper. In China and Japan, where both paper and light are considered sacred, each serves and sets off the other beautifully. Translucent paper diffuses

Other than wall coverings, paper assumes a number of guises in the home. One of the most versatile is paper for the table – cloths, place mats, and napkins – which can be as plain or as pretty as you wish. Among our favorites are the botanical napkins inspired by the art collection at the Victoria & Albert Museum in London, BELOW, designed by IHR in Germany and distributed in the U.S. by Boston International; we've carried them ever since the store opened in 1988.

light; light, in turn, illuminates the subtle shadings and textures of paper. A simple translucent screen banks light so that it is dispersed evenly throughout a room. Light may also be cupped by a lantern or diffused through a shade. One of the earliest devices for defining or setting off an area of a room, and for filtering light, was the screen. Like so many items mentioned in this book, screens originated in China, some two thousand years ago, where they served as a medium for creating zones of privacy within a larger, more open area. Chinese screens were huge and cumbersome; crafted of wood and standing as much as ten feet tall, many measured as long as twenty panels across. When the Japanese adapted the screen to their own striking and idiosyncratic architectural concerns, they distilled it to two lightweight elements: a spare wooden frame filled in with translucent handmade paper.

The Japanese also redefined the functions of the screen and constructed it accordingly. The largest type, a movable partition on feet called a *fusama*, originated to set off a sleeping or resting space from the rest of a room. The *byobu*, a folding screen numbering no more than six panels, is, by contrast, small and portable and unfolds in either direction upon ingeniously engineered hinges. The *byobu* (protection from the wind) can be transported from one location to another to buffer against drafts. Both the *fusama* and the *byobu* are translucent so that light may penetrate what might otherwise be shadowy areas of the house. *Shoji* screens are used in place of glass-paned windows.

In the Far East, the lantern is equated with the soul. Responsive to the slightest movement, a lantern connects human beings to nature, to the seasons, and to the earth. Since their invention in the early fourteenth century in Japan, when candles replaced torches and fish-oil lamps as a primary source of light, lanterns have been used in as many situations as size and shape permit. Some are purely symbolic; others are decorative; still others serve a religious function. *Andon*, for example, were boxlike lanterns constructed upon a wooden frame with feet and hangers; today, and, in a variety of

The symbolic purpose of translucent paper is to create a sense of diffusion, as opposed to aggression. At Mirezi, a restaurant in Manhattan, the partition behind the sake bar is made of saa paper from Thailand with bamboo leaf inclusions.

SOME SHOJI SCREENS

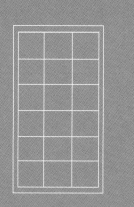

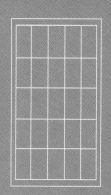

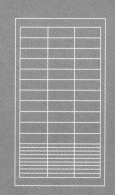
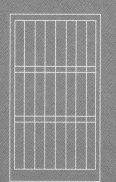

"THE JAPANESE ARE TELLING THE TRUTH WHEN THEY SAY THAT THEIR HOUSE BREATHES AND TREMBLES WITH THEM. THE HUMANITY OF THEIR ENVIRONMENT IS LARGELY CONDITIONED BY THE NATURE OF PAPER."

–DOMINIQUE BUISSON, **THE ART OF JAPANESE PAPER**

shapes, this type of lantern includes *bombori*, which are used to illuminate interiors. *Toro*, inscribed with temple sayings, are reserved for religious use. During purification ceremonies they are floated on water. Enormous paper lanterns made of a ceremonial paper called *nebuta* are carried through the streets in the festival that anticipates harvest. *Nebuta* paper lanterns take the shapes of animals and birds, and sometimes human form. To celebrate the Buddhist Festival of the Dead, ancestral spirits are invoked and heralded with strings of paper lanterns. Folding lanterns called *chochin*, designed to guide those who had to travel about from place to place at night, were, at one time, status objects that had to submit to strict legislation as to their use. A person could be identified by the lantern he carried. The shape and individual markings of a particular lantern revealed its bearer, be he a samurai, a tradesman, or a monk. For women, miniature versions of the *chochin* could slip into the

sleeve of a kimono. Because of their folds, *chochin* today are made by craftsmen adept at making parasols. When not in use, *chochin* reside in boxes made especially to house them.

Decorative lanterns assume a variety of shapes, of which the oblong, gourd, sleeve, and box shapes are the most prevalent. Some stand upon metal feet; others may be suspended from a hanger. Traditionally, all were lit from within by candles. During his lifetime, Isamu Noguchi (1904–88), a Japanese-American sculptor of considerable international renown, devoted a great deal of time and energy to the design and production of a series of lamps he called *akari*—or

At Kate's Paperie, many papers, such as the bark paper opposite, are culled from species of vegetation that renew themselves easily. We also get excited by new uses for paper, such as those slung over dowels at Honmura An, a Japanese noodle restaurant near the shop. Like our paper-wrapped candles, they diffuse light.

Lanie Kagan, of Luz Lampcraft in New York City, trained as an artist and graphic designer before turning her hand to lamps (see three small photos). From the hundreds of papers she collects, she lets the inherent qualities of each paper determine the final design. Rigidity, translucency, and texture all conjoin to influence the shape the lamp will assume; some paper can only be rolled into cylinders.

"light" sculptures. Invited by the mayor of the Japanese city of Gifu to help revitalize the local papermaking industry, Noguchi developed a series of lanternlike lamps that would accommodate an electric lightbulb rather than a candle. Still manufactured by hand in Gifu (and widely copied), the one hundred different *akari* lamps that follow Noguchi's original designs are composed of delicate armatures of bamboo and wire upon which thin, translucent *washi* paper has been pressed. The tallest *akari* lamp spirals from floor to ceiling; the most diminutive ones stand upon a table, shelf, or floor. *Akari* are not only sources of light; they are works of art.

In Korea, much of daily life is lived on the floor. Meals are taken on cushions that encircle a low table; padded mattresses covered with quilts are used for sleeping. To keep warm during their frigid winters, the Koreans devised an ingenious method of radiant heat. To vent smoke and excess heat from their cooking fires, they created a system of flues that ran under the floor from the fire pit to the outdoors. The Koreans then covered the warm floor with a heavy, oiled paper called *changpanji*; the room was thus heated, through the *changpanji*, from the ground up. Both cooking and heating systems have been updated in modern times, but the heating system continues to function in a similar manner. Instead of hot air, though, warmed water circulates through a system of pipes installed beneath the floors. Floor paper continues to be made, both in the traditional manner, by hand, and by machine. The quality of the paper is measured by its weight and thickness. Machine papers are paste veneered in two-, three-, or four-ply thicknesses, then pounded to flatten and strengthen them. Pounding also burnishes the surface and prepares it for the oiling, which adds a luster that ages from a pale yellow tint to amber.

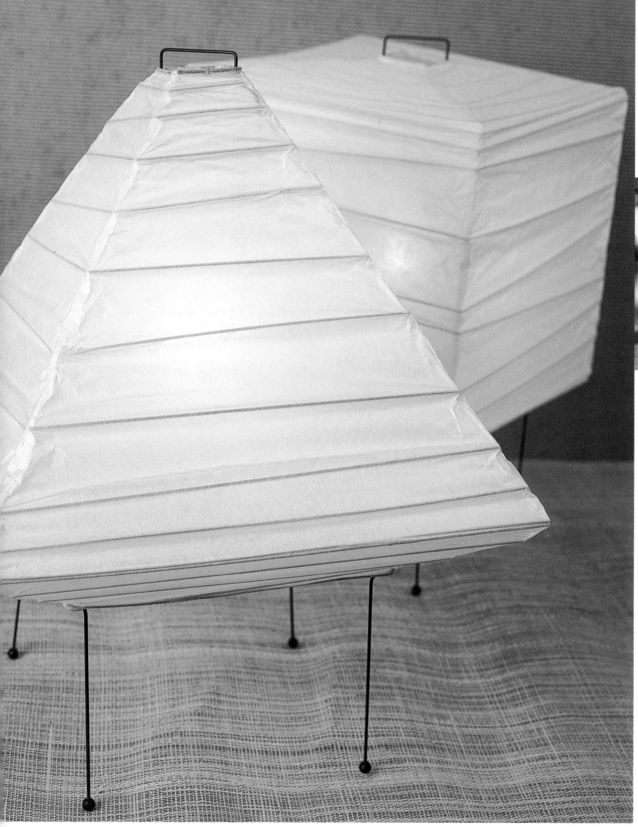

Noguchi's **akari** lamps LEFT set the stage for many practitioners of the art of lamp making. OVERLEAF: At Kate's Paperie, we often suspend a canopy beneath our zigzag paper ceiling to mark a special occasion. This particular canopy, though, was quilted from lots of different papers to deliver a simpler message: to alert everyone who passed underneath to the origins of these and other papers they would find in our shop.

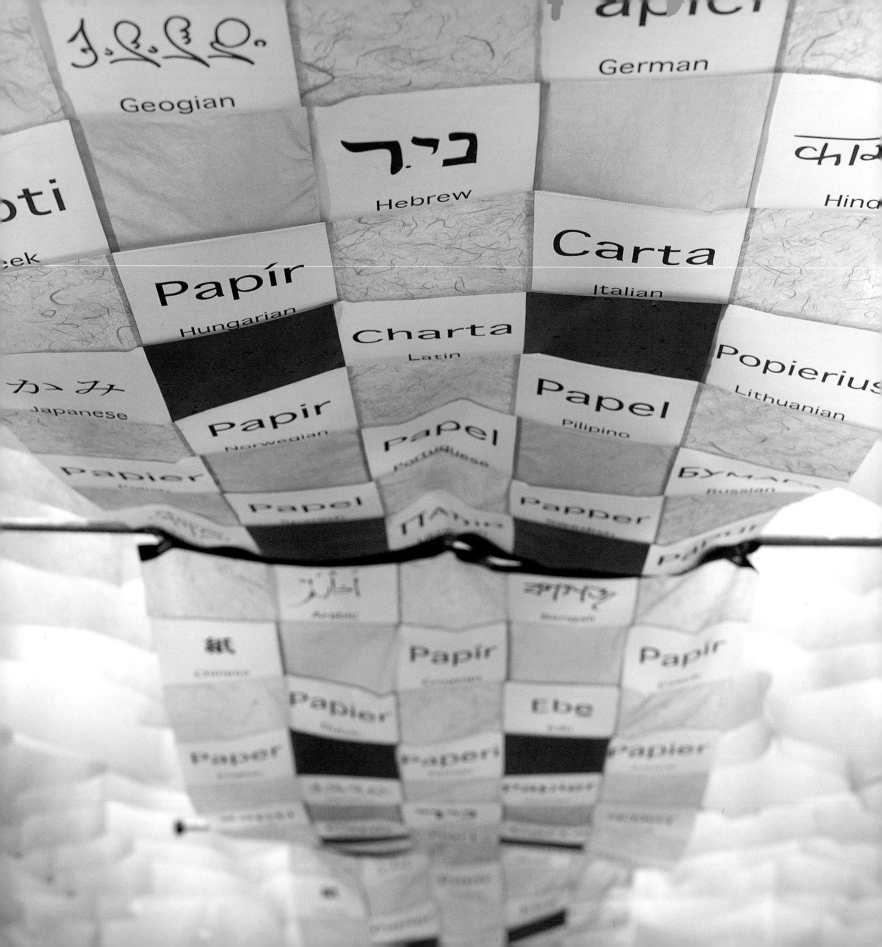

"THERE IS SOMETHING REMARKABLE ABOUT PAPER!
THERE ARE DEAD PAPERS — SOUL-LESS!
THERE ARE INSPIRED ONES.
THIN CHINESE PAPER
MADE FROM TENDER BAMBOO,
MEANT TO BE CONVEYED BY CARRIER PIGEONS;
ARABIC PAPER TREATED WITH SAFFRON;
PERSIAN PAPER SMOOTHED BY HAND,
FIRM OPAQUE EUROPEAN PAPER
GLAZED BETWEEN STEEL ROLLERS;
SUN-BLEACHED OR CHLORINE-BLEACHED PAPER;
PAPER MADE OF THE FIBERS
FROM THE COCOONS OF THE SILKWORM,
SO FINE THAT THEY SEEM ON THE VERGE
OF DISSOLVING INTO NOTHINGNESS
JUST AS A WINE IS FASHIONED,
NOT ONLY BY THE MANNER OF ITS PREPARATION
BUT ALSO BY THE TYPE OF GRAPE
AND THE SOIL IN WHICH IT IS RIPENED,
SO PAPER DEPENDS ON THE SPECIES OF FIBER
AND THE PLACE WHERE IT GREW."

SWEDISH ARTIST RUNE HAGBERG

KATE'S PAPERIE SOHO
561 Broadway
New York, NY 10012
212 941 9816

KATE'S PAPERIE
8 West 13th Street
New York, NY 10011
212 633 0570

KATE'S PAPERIE
1282 Third Avenue
New York, NY 10021
212 396 3670

PAPERMILLS ASSOCIATED WITH KATE'S PAPERIE

ABHINAV, INDIA
Handmade and silkscreened giftwrap paper, many made from reclaimed cotton fibers from the Indian textile industry

AWAGAMI FACTORY, JAPAN
Machine-made and handmade decorative, writing, and printing paper

ECHIZEN WASHI, JAPAN
Machine-made decorative and printing paper

GIFTSLAND ENTERPRISES, NEPAL
Handmade decorative paper

GSG INDUSTRIES, PHILIPPINES
Handmade decorative and art paper

KUANG TAI, THAILAND
Handmade and machine-made printing and decorative paper

MOKUBA, JAPAN
Machine-made wrapping paper

NISHIDA WAFUDO, JAPAN
Machine-made and silkscreened decorative and wrapping paper

OJI PAPER, JAPAN
Machine-made printing and decorative paper

ROYAL CRAFT, THAILAND
Machine-made art and decorative paper

SIAMPHOMPRATHAN, THAILAND
Handmade decorative paper

TOP PRO, THAILAND
Machine-made and handmade paper

TOSA WASHI, JAPAN
Handmade decorative paper

AMALFI, ITALY
100 percent cotton handmade printing and
writing paper

ALCANTARA, ITALY
Handmade art and printing paper

ARJO WIGGINS, FRANCE
Machine-made and mold-made art, printing,
and writing paper

BOCKINGFORD, ENGLAND
Machine-made watercolor paper

CAL'OLIVER MOLI PAPERER, SPAIN
Handmade paper

CARTOTECNICA FIOCCARDI, ITALY
Machine-made decorative paper and boards
(especially recycled paper)

CHARTHAM, ENGLAND
Machine-made printing and writing paper

FABRIANO, ITALY
Machine-made and mold-made paper for art,
writing, and printing

FACZUO, FRANCE
Machine-made recycled printing paper

FRIDOFLACK, SWITZERLAND
Machine-made printing paper

LARROQUE, FRANCE
Handmade art and decorative paper

MUSEO MOLI PAPERER, SPAIN
Handmade decorative, art, and writing paper

ZANDERS, SWITZERLAND
Machine-made printing paper

ZERKALL, GERMANY
Machine-made printing paper

BARBARA LOGAN PAPERWORKS,
UNITED STATES
Handmade decorative and floral inclusion
papers

CRANE'S, UNITED STATES
Machine-made printing and writing papers
made from 100 percent cotton

EVANESCENT PRESS, UNITED STATES
Handmade decorative ecofriendly papers made
from "alternative" papermaking fibers

FRENCH, UNITED STATES
Machine-made printing and writing papers

FOX RIVER, UNITED STATES
Machine-made printing and writing papers

GILBERT, UNITED STATES
Machine-made printing and writing papers

JAMES RIVER, UNITED STATES
Machine-made printing and writing papers

JERUSALEM PAPERWORKS, UNITED STATES
Handmade cotton and recycled decorative
papers

LANGDELL PAPERWORKS, UNITED STATES
Handmade cotton and recycled decorative papers

ST. ARMAND, CANADA
Handmade and mold-made decorative papers
and converted products

STRATHMORE, UNITED STATES
Machine-made printing and writing papers

TWINROCKER, UNITED STATES
Handmade art and decorative paper and
stationery

COSTA RICAN NATURAL PAPER, COSTA RICA
Machine-made writing paper and stationery
made with ecofriendly fibers

LIL MENA PAPER, COSTA RICA
Ecofriendly handmade decorative papers

PAPELES ARTISTICOS DEPONTE, MEXICO
Handmade decorative and art papers

THE AUTHOR WISHES
TO GRATEFULLY ACKNOWLEDGE
THE FOLLOWING SOURCES
FOR PERMISSION
TO REPRODUCE ILLUSTRATIONS
ON THE PAGES NOTED:

□ □ □

Collection of Eric Baker: pp. 60–61, 76–77 □ Crane & Co., Dalton, Massachusetts: pp. 6, 26, 57, 59, 84, 85, 112 (left), 116 □ *Diderot Encyclopedia, The Complete Illustrations*, vol. 1: p. 93 (*Proportions d'une Plume taillée*) □ Dover Pictorial Archives: pp. 51 (from *The Book of Trades* by Jost Amman and Hans Sachs), 68–69 (from *Diderot Pictorial Encyclopedia of Trades & Industry*), 110 (from *Diderot Pictorial Encyclopedia of Trades & Industry*), 174 (from *William Morris Full Color Patterns and Designs*) □ Fabriano Italia, Fabriano, Italy: pp. 28, 48 □ Fine Art Photographic Library, London/Art Resource, New York, p. 94 (*The Love Letter* by Charles Soulacroix, Anthony Mitchell Fine Paintings, Nottingham, Great Britain) □ Fine Lines Handmarbled Papers, Connecticut: p. 130 (Turkish Stone Papers by Nelle Tresselt) □ Ian Harkness, Texas: p. 130 (Cockerell Papers by Ann Muir) □ Honmura An Restaurant, New York, New York: p. 177 □ Kate's Paperie, 561 Broadway, New York, New York: pp. 14, 22–23, 182 □ Koho School of Sumie, New York, New York: p. 45 □ Mi Cocina Restaurant, New York, New York: p. 141 □ Mirezi Restaurant, New York, New York: p. 174 □ Newark Museum, Newark, New Jersey/Art Resource New York: p. 143 (*Lady Offering Man a Small Green Box*, Shundo Katsukawa [c. 1790], characters from the drama of the Forty-seven Ronin) □ The Pierpont Morgan Library/Art Resource New York: pp. 40 (Tavara Monastery, Spain, A.D. 1220, M.429, f.183), 41 (Latin Bible, 13–14th century Italy, M.436, f.319v), 66 (detail of the Biblia Latina, Mainz, Gutenberg & Fust, c. 1455, vol. 11, f.131v–132, PML 818) □ Research Institute of Paper History & Technology, Carriage House, Brookline, Massachusetts: p. 34 (*Tibetan Monks* by Sidney Koretsky) □ Robert C. Williams American Museum of Papermaking: pp. 32, 112 (right), 113